The
Ferry
Home

To Ted,

Enjoy the journey!

Debbie Kasman Tillinghast

The
Ferry
Home

A MEMOIR

Debbie Kaiman Tillinghast

Editors: Christian Pacheco, Donna Melillo, Kayte Middleton
Cover Design: Jason Kauffmann/Firelight Interactive/firelightinteractive.com
Interior Design and Layout: Rick Soldin
Back Cover Photo: Pat Kenny
Map: Printed with the permission of the Prudence Island Historical & Preservation Society.

Indigo River Publishing
3 West Garden Street Ste. 352
Pensacola, FL 32502
www.indigoriverpublishing.com

Ordering Information:
Quantity sales: Special discounts are available on quantity purchases by corporations, associations, and others. For details, contact the publisher at the address above.

Orders by U.S. trade bookstores and wholesalers: Please contact the publisher at the address above.

Printed in the United States of America

Publisher's Cataloging-in-Publication Data is available upon request.

Library of Congress Control Number: 2015947694

ISBN: 978-0-9962330-1-9

First Edition

*With Indigo River Publishing, you can always expect great
books, strong voices, and meaningful messages.
Most importantly, you'll always find ... words worth reading.*

—•—

This book is dedicated to my parents Sol and Evelyn, whose love for each other was a constant steadying force in my life.

To my grandmother Emmie, who not only loved me unconditionally, but also infused in me so much of herself.

To my sister, Pat, my one truly forever friend.

To my three children, Eric, Peter, and Adam, and my grandchildren, Ethan, Evelyn, Oliver, Owen, and my future grandchildren, whose love continues to sustain me. May you each find the island spirit that dwells within you. All my love to each of you.

—•—

Contents

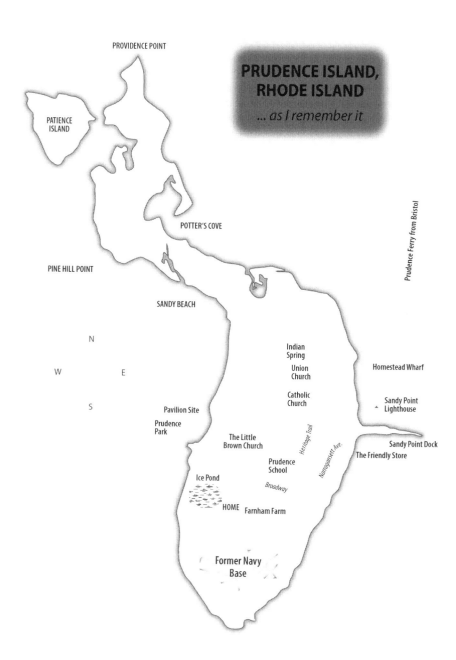

PROVIDENCE POINT

PATIENCE
ISLAND

**PRUDENCE ISLAND,
RHODE ISLAND**

... as I remember it

POTTER'S COVE

PINE HILL POINT

Prudence Ferry from Bristol

SANDY BEACH

N

W   E

S

Indian
Spring

Union
Church

Homestead Wharf

Catholic
Church

Pavilion Site

Sandy Point
Lighthouse

Prudence
Park

The Little
Brown Church

Heritage Trail

Prudence
School

Narragansett Ave.

Sandy Point Dock
The Friendly Store

Ice Pond

Broadway

HOME   Farnham Farm

**Former Navy
Base**

Acknowledgments

Writing is a solitary endeavor, much like living on an island. Yet, bringing a book to life requires a community of support, which is also essential for island living. This book would not have been possible without the encouragement of my community of support. My love and gratitude go to Judy Little, who offered not only her sustaining friendship and excitement, but also her Prudence Island home as a quiet spot to reconnect with my memories.

I also give special thanks to the writing class at my local library, composed of leader Pat Kenny and participants Barbara, George, and Judy. Without their positive reception, my passion for Prudence might never have become a book. The challenge of converting my written words to print was aided by my friend Sandy, who typed all the initial pages, spurring me on in the process with her enthusiasm.

Thank you, Barbara, Dean, Elizabeth, Janet, Kathy, Lynne, and Stephen for your time and insight serving as test readers. I am grateful to friend and author Wayne Reilly, who frequently encouraged me to write a book about Prudence Island. I am also indebted to the Prudence Island community of long ago as well as the present one who continues to welcome me today.

Finally, my enduring love and appreciation go to my son Adam, who assisted and guided me every step of the way, providing motivation and inspiration when needed and ultimately making this dream become a reality. I consider this book a gift that was given to me, and I am grateful for the opportunity to share it with you, my family, friends, and anyone one who has ever loved Prudence Island or any special childhood spot that lives on in your memory. May it connect you with or help you embark on your own journey home.

A Place of Peace

T he soft voice of the yoga teacher draws the class to a close. "Relax your eyes, your face, your shoulders … go to that special place of peace and relaxation." I close my eyes, and the chanting music fades into the distance, replaced by the quiet music of waves gently lapping the shore on Prudence Island. My breath slows to their soft, steady rhythm, in and out. I am sitting on the rocks on the west side of the island on a warm summer day. The breeze off the water whispers around me, playing with my hair. I feel the sun warm on my face, and my breath matches the ocean's breath. The only sounds are the waves and the occasional high-pitched *chick-ta-ree* of a red-winged blackbird as it calls from a nearby marsh.

Prudence Island is my place of peace and relaxation. It was my first home, and its essence inhabits my heart, my soul, my being. My original thought was to write the memories I have of a Prudence Island childhood for my children and grandchildren because I wanted them to feel a connection to their roots and to the independent spirit living in each of them. As I began writing, I realized that this was only part of the reason—the surface reason—for writing this memoir. The deeper reason was much more personal. I felt a need to reconnect with myself—to find again the inner tranquility and comfort with who I am that came out of island living. I needed to find a part of me that I had lost.

Returning to Prudence as it is today is like traveling through time. As I ride the ferry to the island, I shed accumulated layers of stress and anxiety, like discarding many layers of winter clothing when spring arrives. I step off the ferry feeling lighter, more at peace, and content to just be.

September Sounds

I am looking out on the blue September bay through air as clear as a just-washed window. A solitary sailboat glides by on a light, easterly breeze with the outgoing tide. I am enveloped in the island's post-Labor-Day stillness, where the sounds of children's laughter are now a distant echo. The start of school has carried them away from their summer friends and swimming fun. The sun is still comfortably warm, but the rustle of drying leaves reminds me of balmy September days from my childhood, when the excitement of starting school was mingled with sorrow over summer's end.

—•—

Sue Cummins stood in the center of the school yard, her plaid skirt lifting slightly in the gentle September breeze, and called out to Charlie Brayton, "You may take three giant steps!"

"May I?" asked Charlie.

"No, you may take three *baby* steps."

Charlie inched forward three tiny steps as Sue shouted, "Oh, you have to go back! You forgot to say 'May I?'!"

My first day of school had begun. As more children arrived, they joined the game. That day, it was "giant steps," but another day, it may have been red rover, hide and seek, or one of many variations of tag. I had been longing to go to school for three years, ever since I first saw my older sister Patsy go off each day with our mother, who also happened to be the teacher. At last, I was also there, playing games with the older children until we heard the clanging of the school bell—the signal to end our games and go inside.

There were two entrances to the schoolhouse, one on each side of the front steps. The right one was for the girls, the left for the boys. On warm spring days, entry to the building included a mad dash through the swarms of honeybees that nested under the eaves. Each outside door opened to a coatroom with hooks lining the outside edge. Coats were hung and lunchboxes were left behind as we opened the door to enter the only classroom. We were enveloped by the pervasive aroma of school paste, chalk dust, floor varnish, used books, and the permanent, slightly musty smell of an old building little changed over the years. It was the smell of school.

Wooden desks and chairs of varying sizes were screwed to the floor through their black metal legs. Each desk had a top that lifted to reveal storage space for books, and there was an inkwell nestled in the upper right-hand corner. Across the top was a small valley for securely holding pencils so they wouldn't constantly roll off the slanted desktop into an unsuspecting lap. A large propane stove sat in the front of the room, a recent replacement for the coal stove that previously provided heat. The walls between the side windows held several high, glass-doored bookcases. The closet between the cloakroom doors hid wonderful treasures—various paper and craft supplies, big jars of school paste, and also the thick rope pulled to ring the bell. We all wanted a turn at that job.

When I started school, there was no indoor plumbing. A hand pump in the front yard provided well water, and there were two adjoining outhouses behind the school, one for boys and one for girls. They were painted the same dark green that trimmed the shingled school building. Behind the outhouses stood the remains of the coal pile, no longer needed to supply heat. In spring and fall, the outhouses were a source not only of a potent fragrance, but also of many wasps and spiders. I didn't care to deal with any of that. Instead I preferred the coal pile, which was out in the fresh air and wasp-free. I did have to be stealthy and fleet of foot though, and I was constantly scrutinizing the back windows to make sure no one was watching as I made my dash *behind* the outhouse.

An addition, including a furnace room, two bathrooms, and a large hallway for storage, was built onto the school in 1953. In fact, the addition was almost as big as the original building. Since running water and flush toilets were added, the outhouse and coal pile were no longer needed. While the construction was being completed, school was held in the recreation hall of my father's store. New desks had been purchased in advance for the renovated building, and they provided a bit of schoolroom atmosphere as well as practical work space for our school day. We missed the grassy yard and woods for our recess play, but the boardwalk along the store was fine for some games, and others could be played in the dirt road leading to the store.

The day began as we sat at our desks, heads bowed, reciting the Lord's Prayer. That was followed by the Pledge of Allegiance and then health inspection. Each student received a turn to be "health inspector," the role changing weekly. The designated child moved from desk to desk checking to see if shoes were tied, hair was combed, hands and fingernails were clean, and finally, if breakfast was eaten and teeth were brushed that morning. If everything were perfect, a score of five was reported to and recorded by my mother. I liked being health inspector because then I didn't have to display my hands for inspection. I had severe eczema, which resulted in misshapen fingernails that grew in bumps and ridges, and keeping them clean and neat was not only a constant challenge but also a source of daily embarrassment.

After health inspection, we sang four or five songs with my mother accompanying us on the piano. We each had a songbook and would eagerly wave a hand, hoping for a chance to request our favorite. "My Grandfather's Clock" and "The Giant and the Hill" were two of mine.

Once a giant came a-wandering late at night when the
*   world was still,*
Seeking for a stool to sit on, he climbed a little green hill.
When he reached the highest part of it, sat him down
*   on its very peak.*
The Little Hill cried out in a faint and far away squeak:

Giant giant, I am under you,
Move or this is the last of me!
But the giant answered,
Thank you! I like it here, don't you see?

Sometimes, instead of starting the day with singing, my mother would lead a few folk dances for the music portion of our day. Although I liked to dance, I always hoped she would choose dances that didn't require holding hands because the other children often refused to hold mine. I repeatedly told them that my eczema was not contagious, but they were still deterred by my reddened hands, which sometimes bore open sores. At those moments, I hated folk dancing and my hands as well, but I tried to appear indifferent and pretend it didn't matter.

Some years, every grade from kindergarten through eighth grade was represented in our school; other years, there might be gaps or no one past the sixth grade. In 1952, when there was a polio epidemic on the mainland, the school was full. Parents preferred to have their children in the relatively germ-free environment of Prudence Island, so summer residents stayed past Labor Day until they felt it was safe to return home.

Every Monday morning, my mother met with each child and gave out individual assignments for the week, which were written on lined paper, one subject per line. We worked independently, at our own pace, and my mother supplied help and direction as needed. Also, the older students often helped the younger ones. The one requirement was that we completed all the assigned work by the end of the school day on Friday. As I finished each subject, I crossed it off with a different colored crayon, completely filling the space between the lines, and by Friday afternoon I had a lovely rainbow for a reward. Some students chose to do an assignment from each subject every day, but I had a different approach. I loved math, and that is how I spent every Monday; so by the end of the day, my math assignments had the badge of completion—a brightly colored stripe.

I worked my way through the week, completing all my favorites first, a day at a time. This was a great system—that is, until Friday afternoon arrived, and everything was done except a whole week's assignments of the dreaded reading workbook! I loved to read, but alas, I hated answering all the questions in the workbook. More than one Friday afternoon found me staying after school with my mother until I finished every single workbook assignment. The reward when all our assignments were done early was free time to play with blocks and games, read a book, or enjoy making the crafts that were available. I liked to make intricate cutout paper designs and then place that design on another piece of paper and fill it in, recreating my lacy pattern in vibrant color.

One Friday afternoon when I was in fourth grade, Bobby Edwards, the only other fourth grader, and I had both finished our work for the week. We were trying to think of something to do while my mother continued to work with the other students. I came up with the idea of putting a block on Bobby's head and then throwing dominoes at it to knock it off. This was great fun until I missed the block and hit him in the head instead. He was not happy, and I quickly changed the game before he could make too much of a fuss! I didn't think any more about it until that evening when Mrs. Edwards called my mother and said Bobby had a dent in his head, which he thought was from being hit by a domino. My mother had mixed thoughts and feelings about the situation. She couldn't believe that a domino would have left a dent in Bobby Edwards' very hard head, and although she didn't't say so to Mrs. Edwards, she thought the dent had probably been there all along. However, she was NOT happy about this game being played when her back was turned.

When she had calmed down Mrs. Edwards, my mother hung up the phone and asked me whose idea it was to play that game. I had to confess that it was my idea and not Bobby's. She said she would have understood if it were his idea, but she had trouble accepting the fact that I, who she thought was responsible, would come up with such a game. Oh dear, the shame I felt! I wasn't worried about Bobby Edward's head. I was pretty sure I had felt that dent on another occasion when I ran my hand over his short brush cut to see how it felt—I was pretty sure his head was naturally dented. But I had disappointed my mother! She thought she could trust me to use my free time appropriately, and I had let her down.

The dominoes game was not the only time my behavior was less than stellar. The first such incident occurred when I was in kindergarten. My mother was reading to a group of us, and I let out a loud shout—for no particular reason except I wanted to hear my own voice, and I wondered what would happen. Needless to say, I quickly found out! My mother was very cross. My father was called to come pick me up from school early that day, and on the ride back he asked me why I was being sent home.

"Mommy was angry," was my response.

"Why was she angry?" he pressed.

I looked right at him, and said, "I have no idea."

That was surely not the answer he was expecting, but his only comment was, "Mommy must have had a reason, and I'll find out anyway when she comes home."

I refrained from wading any deeper into the pool of trouble I had created. I knew punishment was looming on the horizon for the evening, but in the meantime I would just enjoy the extra time at home with my grandmother.

— • —

The afternoon brings the incoming tide and a fresh, westerly breeze as the lone sailboat floats by, returning home from its day of adventure. The sun has lost its warmth, and the chilly wind is a reminder of brisk autumn days on the cusp of summer and winter days that are just waiting for their turn. I go inside to retrieve my favorite purple sweatshirt and sit outside once more, watching the sun slip quietly into the bay.

A Princess and a Clown

The swamp maples have already turned fiery red, and the leaf tips of the sugar maples are brushed with orange. My roses are still happily blooming, but the grass glistens white with a light, premature frost on this chilly end-of-summer morning. My son and his wife are here visiting from Florida, where they miss the crisp fall days of their roots, and we have decided to go apple-picking. By the time we arrive at the orchard soon after lunch, the sun has regained a portion of its heat. The sweet fragrance of the sun-warmed apples mingles with the rich, jammy smell of concord grapes growing wild in the woods that skirt the orchard. An abundance of bright orange pumpkins sit

together, patiently waiting to be chosen. They range in size from tiny ones as small as a teacup all the way to a round one that is as big as an exercise ball. It would make a perfect whimsical stool, even for an adult.

As I survey the pumpkins and make my selection, I think ahead to Halloween, but the childhood memories it sparks are not of pumpkins, but other things.

—•—

The children sat in a circle, their eyes covered with blindfolds, as Louise Cummins told her gruesome story, "A black cat ran in front of Pete when he was on his way to the party, and he ran over it with the car. This is what was left. Here are the two eyeballs." The eyes were passed from child to child, and their slimy roundness was met by squeals of fascinated horror. Next came the intestines and then a paw as the squeals continued. We were at the Prudence Island Halloween Party, and when our blindfolds were removed, the various parts came around again: two peeled grapes, a bowl of cold spaghetti, and a fake rabbit's foot from a keychain.

Halloween was an exciting time on the island. There was no candy-laden trick or treating, but we had costumes and glorious parties. One party was held at the school just for the children. Black cats, big orange pumpkins with triangular eyes and noses, and witches flying across the moon decorated all the windows. Orange and black crepe paper streamers looped around the room, as we had worked all week making decorations to transform the school. We all sat in our costumes, struggling to get through a morning of schoolwork as we anticipated the afternoon party. My mother planned a variety of games for us: relay races, bobbing for apples, musical chairs, and dropping clothespins into a bottle. There were always prizes for the winners, and of course there would be prizes for the best costumes, too.

When my mother gave costume prizes at the school party, I knew I would not be the recipient of any because she didn't want to show that she favored me. One year, she made little chocolate loaf cakes to give as prizes, and I so wanted one of them! She had frosted them with orange frosting and decorated them with frosting pumpkins and licorice black cats. As much as I longed for one, I knew that prize was not to be mine.

On Halloween night, the island party was held in the recreation hall at my dad's store. Everyone on the island came, adults and children alike, and almost everyone wore a costume. One year, Dr. Priscilla Selman came as Salome, complete with John the Baptist's head on a platter. Living on an island fosters an interesting sense of humor.

My sister and I were required to take an unwelcome nap that afternoon, as we would inevitably be awake way past our bedtime. There were always games at this party, too, and the adults joined in along with the children. We would bob for apples, and doughnuts were hung from the ceiling by strings. They would see who could eat the most doughnuts from these swaying strings in the allotted time—but no hands were allowed. I could never eat mine fast enough to win. Marshmallows were placed in the center of a long string. Two people, with opposite ends of the string in their mouths and hands held behind their backs, would try to eat their way up the string to see who would reach the marshmallow first, and the person who was successful got to eat the marshmallow. I loved this game since I loved marshmallows, and I was often the marshmallow-eating victor.

We formed teams for various relay races, carrying a hard-boiled egg on a spoon or a newspaper relay where two people worked together, one moving the newspaper across the floor a step at a time so the walker's feet never touched the floor. My favorite was the suitcase relay. Each team had two suitcases filled with clothes, one for a man and one for a woman. Pairs from each team ran to the designated spot, and the man would put on the woman's clothes and the woman, the man's. They would then run back, take off the clothes, put them in the suitcase, and hand them off to the next pair. Since there were always outlandish combinations, it was fun to watch even if you weren't participating. One time, all the women and girls put one of their shoes in a pile on the floor. At the signal, all the men and boys ran up and reached into the pile to grab a shoe. The person who matched his shoe to the owner first got a prize, as did the owner of the shoe.

There was also dancing with music provided by the island band, who sat on the stage at one end of the hall. Todd Farnham played the guitar and sometimes sang with his Southern cowboy twang. Lester Grant played the fiddle, Roger Grant played the piano, Benny Brayton played the trumpet, and my dad played the drums. This eclectic band also performed every year for the Firemen's Ball, which was held at the end of summer. Tables and chairs outlined the hall to leave room for dancing and games in the middle. The refreshment tables were laden with goodies, including sandwiches cut in crustless triangular quarters, brownies, Rice Krispie treats, sugar cookies that looked like pumpkins, and bowls of popcorn and candy corn. There was apple cider, coffee, and hot chocolate— something to please any palate.

The band provided music for the highlight of the evening: the costume parade. All the costumed children and adults would parade in a circle, and the judges would be chosen from those remaining seated around the hall. At the end of the evening, prizes were awarded in a variety of categories including the scariest, funniest, most original, and prettiest. The categories were limited only by the judges' creativity. When the prizes were given out, I was always hopeful. Even though I didn't consistently win a prize, at least I knew I had a chance to win at the island party.

One year, my mother made me a clown costume. She took a big bolt of white and red striped fabric that she had tucked away in the trunk and made a colorful clown outfit. It was full and baggy with elastic at the neck, wrists, and ankles to make ruffles. There were three big red pompoms marching down the front. She made a hat as well, forming cardboard into a cone shape and covering it with the same red and white striped fabric. Another big red pompom perched on the top of it, and thin, covered elastic under my chin held the hat in place. I didn't win a prize that year, even though I knew the costume was equal to that worn by any circus clown. My sister, however, did win a prize for the scariest costume. She was a witch and wore a black cape over a black dress and carried a broom in her hand. The costume was completed by a grotesque rubber mask on her face with a hooked nose and huge warts.

The next year, I was a princess. My mother made my dress from an old lavender drapery. The material was soft and silky and fell gracefully to my ankles. It had a scooped neck with elastic running through it and puffy sleeves. Elastic nipped in the waistline, and the original scallop border on the drapery provided the decoration on the bottom. I wore my best black patent leather shoes, which were normally saved for church, and ruffled white ankle socks. The final touch was a string of pearls worn in my hair for a crown, and I just knew mine was the most beautiful costume ever. I glided around the costume parade with my head held high, and when the prizes were given out, I was awarded the prize for the prettiest costume!

—•—

I arrive back home from the orchard with tart Cortland apples to make a pie, and it now bubbles in the oven, giving off the sweet perfume of cinnamon, apples, and brown sugar. It will be the ideal ending to our almost-fall day. I also secured a perfectly round orange pumpkin, the size of a basketball, which is now sitting on my doorstep. These days, there are no longer any trick-or-treaters knocking on my door nor have I held a Halloween costume party or bobbed for apples in many years. Nevertheless, I will carve this pumpkin into a jack-o-lantern for all the goblin ghosts of my childhood Halloweens.

.

Sol and Mrs. Kaiman

This morning, I wake to the sound of dripping water. An ice dam on the roof has caused a leak, and a search for the source leads me to the upstairs hall closet. I realize I must empty this small, room-sized storage depot to determine the extent of the damage. As I reach into the far corner behind a bureau, my hand finds a black metal box decorated with antique pink roses. I lift the hinged cover and discover three autograph albums that belonged to my mother. The leak is forgotten as I turn the pages of the first book, captivated by the whimsical rhymes and sayings that are still clearly legible. The book is a keepsake from 1930, when my mother attended Camp Vail, a regional 4-H camp in Vermont. I pause after reading this entry:

> Love many
> Trust few
> Always paddle your own canoe.

It was written by a camper named Ida Compton, and I wonder if she knew even then that my mother did paddle her own canoe, and the one person she trusted implicitly was my dad.

— • —

"How did you meet?" Not an unusual question at social gatherings, but one that always delighted my mother. She would anticipate the wide-eyed, slack-jawed response when she would answer with a twinkle in her eye, "In a mental hospital."

My mother, Evelyn Cornelia Patience Herlein, was born on Patience Island, Rhode Island. She lived there until she was old enough to start school, at which point the family moved to Prudence Island. The Prudence school only went as far as the eighth grade, so when it was time to go to high school, she lived during the week with her older brother George and his wife in Newport, Rhode Island. He owned a variety store called Tarbox, I believe, where he made his own ice cream. My mother worked there through high school, returning to Prudence only on the weekends.

Meeting her for the first time, you might have seen a gracious lady with a warm and friendly smile, but under the reserved and proper exterior lived a wonderful sense of humor and an iron will. Like a mill pond, whose surface is peacefully serene, beneath that quiet calm was a depth and determination that took her on journeys uncommon for a woman in the 1930s—especially for a woman who grew up on two tiny islands in Narragansett Bay. She became active in 4-H while she was in high school, and her dream was to go to college to become a 4-H agent. Undeterred by the scarcity of money or the fact that higher education for women at that time was rare, she attended Rhode Island State College—now the University of Rhode Island—majoring in home economics. She financed her education by summer work and living with the Gilbert family during the year, where she cooked, cleaned, and cared for their two children in exchange for room and board.

While she was in college, she met and fell in love with a young man named Carl Gary, who was already a 4-H agent. She thought she had met her future husband, and Carl made frequent trips to Prudence, even joining in on a family vacation trip. Then one day, Carl met Helen, who was to become his wife. My mother said her heart was broken, but she also said that later she was so glad it had happened, as she otherwise would not have met my dad.

Solomon Mason Kaiman, my dad, was born in Patterson, New Jersey to Ukrainian immigrant parents. I grew up thinking he was Russian, but have learned in recent years that the family was Ukrainian instead. He grew up in Brooklyn as the oldest of seven children. His dad was a barber by trade, and his mother, coming from a more aristocratic and wealthy background, had no means of earning a living. There was very little detail when my dad talked about his growing up. He always tried to find something funny to make us laugh, and he usually had a story about being champion at whatever game we might be playing at the time, whether jacks, marbles, or hopscotch.

My dad's father eventually deserted the family, and the children were put in an orphanage because their mother couldn't support them. The younger ones went to foster homes, but this was not true for my dad, as nobody wanted a teenage foster child. He lived in the orphanage until he was sixteen, when he was subsequently turned out on the street. He stowed away on a ship sailing out of New York Harbor so he would have a place to live, and he worked off his passage until the ship returned. I never learned this about him until long after he died and my Aunt Dotty visited from California. Had I known about his childhood, perhaps it would have helped me understand him and his temper that was often so quick and so harsh.

Somewhere along the way, he not only learned to swim, but he also became an excellent swimmer, attending UCLA on a swimming scholarship. I wish I knew exactly how that transpired, but it speaks to his formidable determination as well as his intelligence, as he was studying to be a doctor. During his years at UCLA, he was an alternate for the Olympic swim team and swam with Buster Crabbe and Johnny Weissmuller, one of the earliest Tarzans. Sadly, his scholarship ran out due to the Depression. He joined the CCC and helped to build the Hoover Dam, and then he continued to take whatever jobs he could find as he worked his way back across the country.

My mother graduated from the University of Rhode Island in 1935, but her dream didn't end there. She worked for a year and then went to Columbia University, working toward a master's degree in physical education. Her money also ran out, but she was able to find a job as a recreational therapist at a mental hospital in White Plains, New York, where she taught folk dancing and organized activities for the patients. The tall, handsome lifeguard at the hospital was a man named Sol Kaiman. Who would imagine that a Baptist girl from Prudence Island would fall in love with a Jewish boy from Brooklyn? Who would think that a Jewish boy with a troubled past would fall in love with an island girl whose determination was equal to his own? But that is exactly what happened.

They had to keep their romance a secret because fraternizing between hospital employees was not only frowned upon, but forbidden. They would sneak away under the dark of night to meet, and ultimately, they decided to get married. In order to prevent any opposition that might arise from her family, my mother wrote each family member a letter, telling them about my dad and saying that if they had a problem with the marriage, she was sorry, but she was going to marry him anyway. Whenever she told the story, she always ended it by saying, "And of course, they all loved Sol."

They had a secret ceremony with only a Justice of the Peace and two witnesses in attendance. I never heard them mention the people who served as witnesses and whose names appear on the marriage certificate—perhaps they were only acquaintances. Somehow, the hospital did find out that they were married and fired them both on the spot. There they were: newly married, jobless, and without a place to live. They moved back to New York City where they spent their first Thanksgiving together. They invited my dad's family to come to dinner, which explains the odd number of plates even now in my mother's set of dishes. There are nine. That's how many would be at the dinner, so that's how many plates my parents bought. My mother said when it was time to buy the turkey, they measured the small oven in their tiny apartment and bought a roasting pan that would fit in it and then bought a turkey that would fit in the roasting pan.

They eventually moved back to Rhode Island, first to Newport and then to Prudence Island in 1943. My dad was not eligible for active military duty because he suffered from severe stomach ulcers. However, he still wanted to serve the country during the war and worked as a civilian at the Navy base located at the south end of Prudence. They lived with my mother's parents, and when my grandfather died in 1947, my dad took over the running of his store at Sandy Point. In the winter, he worked out on the bay doing bull raking (the process of using large, long-handled tongs to harvest quahogs from the bottom of the bay). It was physically demanding work, especially on raw winter days. My mother was recruited by Mr. Maine, the superintendent of Portsmouth schools, to become the teacher at the Prudence school. She had no teaching experience, but I think she was the only year-round resident on the island with a college degree—thus, in his mind, the most likely candidate.

Once my mother became the schoolteacher, all the children and most adults referred to her as Mrs. Kaiman. No child, even summer children, would ever call the teacher by her first name. As proprietor of the island store, my dad was Sol to everyone. Actually, I can't ever remember anyone calling him Mr. Kaiman, and that suited him just fine. He had an outgoing ease with everyone, accepting people where they were and expecting the same in return. So, he was

Sol to all, adults AND children. I can remember my parents being together in the store, and the customer's greeting to them would be, "Hi, Mrs. Kaiman! Hi, Sol!"

My dad was my mother's champion. He encouraged and supported her as she continued her education and advanced professionally. Once hired as the teacher on Prudence, she went to teachers' college during the summer. After years of teaching, she became a University of Rhode Island Extension Agent and ultimately the State Home Economist. My dad's advanced education came through books and experience. He was a voracious reader, and there was no job he wouldn't tackle. When the store was lost in the 1954 hurricane, he took a job at the *Bristol Phoenix*, a weekly newspaper. He learned everything there was to know about publishing a newspaper, from typesetting to advertising to editing. There was never an issue that she had more formal education than he did, and there was no one prouder than he when she received her master's degree from URI when she was fifty-five years old.

My parents' life was far from constant bliss. I hated to hear them argue. My mother seldom raised her voice while my dad often erupted into angry yelling. My stomach would become a hard, knotted ball inside me, and I would wonder, "*Why doesn't she yell back? Why does she let him speak to her that way?*" I grew up afraid of his quick and unpredictable temper. It wasn't until I was older that I realized those arguments were not a reflection of any lack of love or respect; they were a result of very different, equally strong personalities and styles of expression. My mother's patient calm was a counterpoint to my dad's short-fused passion.

As a child, I didn't see my parents being overly demonstrative of their love, but they were not without occasional affectionate kisses and touches. That affection seemed to grow, not fade over the years. I can remember coming home for a visit after I was married. My parents had recently attended a festive evening with dinner and dancing. I don't remember the occasion, nor do I remember any details that were shared. What I do remember is my dad's closing comment about the evening. He said, "And your mother was the best-looking woman there."

My parents did love to dance. My dad danced like he played the drums, creatively, improvising as he went along. He had an incredible sense of rhythm, but where his feet would travel next, you just never knew. I never did master dancing with my dad, but my mother had no problem at all. In spite of their almost ten-inch difference in height, she would follow him without ever a misstep. She always knew intuitively where he would go next, and they would glide gracefully around the dance floor like one body with four feet. In fact, that is how they went through life—two very different people with an unseen, palpable connection. You couldn't be in their presence for any length of time and not sense the depth of love, respect, and admiration they had for each other.

That bond carried them through the loss of their primary livelihood when my dad's store was destroyed. They spent a year living apart, able to see each other only on weekends, as my dad was on the mainland and my mom was still teaching on Prudence Island. There was no FEMA back then, so they worked together for years to pay back all the debts the loss incurred.

My parents were soul-mates long before it became a familiar term. My mother told me once that my dad was the only person in her entire life to whom she could bare her soul. Although he never spoke the words, I have no doubt that my dad felt the same way. I heard someone say once that a couple went together like peanut butter and jelly. I thought, *"What a simple and beautiful way to say that two people were perfect for each other!"* Well, in my parents' case, perhaps you could say they went together like lox and bagels.

—•—

My mother loved my dad with a passion that lasted until the day she died, twenty-six years after he did. A few days before that, I sat next to her bed holding her hand. She looked at me and said, "I loved your dad so much, and I still miss him." They came from two very different worlds, but the depth of love my parents shared would surely be a blessing in any life. It is this level of shared love and trust that I wish for all my children and grandchildren, as they each paddle their own canoe.

The Little Brown Church

Come to the church in the wildwood,
Oh come to the church in the dale...

I sit in a small Baptist church in the northwest corner of Rhode Island. It is the church attended by my dear friend Nan Campbell, and I have accompanied her here today. The minister's warm greeting and the parishioners' friendly welcome immediately make me feel at home, as if a close-knit family has invited me to join them. The singing of the familiar old hymns "In the Garden" and "Fairest Lord Jesus" awakens memories of the first church I attended on Prudence Island and the warmth and safety that enfolded me there.

— • —

As a child, when I first heard the hymn "The Church in the Wild-wood" sung in the church on the west side of Prudence Island, I was convinced that it was written about our church. Prudence Community Church was a small building with a corner bell tower and grayed, weathered shingles. Heated, but still chilly around the edges in cold weather, it was the winter church for the island. Everyone on the island who wished to attend church came here, regardless of their faith.

The church was quite dark inside because of the brown wood paneling covering the walls and floor. The pews, which lined the center aisle, had seat cushions covered with soft, wine-colored fabric and black iron frames. There was a thin, red carpet running down the aisle to the two front steps that led to the platform holding the pulpit. This level also served as a stage for school and Sunday school performances.

This was the place that provided my first religious education, but more than that, it was a safe place to be. I knew all the people who were there: the Sunday school teacher, the organist, the minister, and all the people in the pews. After Sunday school was over and the church service began, I would snuggle up against my grandmother and sleep through the sermon. There was only one spot in the church that worried me. There was a little room off to the right of the sanctuary, perhaps where the choir might robe if there were a choir or the spot where the children used to don their costumes for a play. Opening off the back of that room was another door, which revealed a very dark room or was maybe the entrance to the cellar. All I knew was that it was a very scary place. I learned one day in Sunday school that Jesus was everywhere, so I asked my mother, "Is Jesus behind that door too?" She assured me that he was. Then, in my childish mind, that was where Jesus lived—in the dark, scary space behind the unknown door. That small lesson of God's presence, even in the dark and scary places, became the foundation of my abiding adult faith.

The women of the church took turns preparing communion on the first Sunday of the month. My sister and I liked it when it was my mother's turn because it meant that at the end of church, we got to eat all the leftover little cubes of crustless bread and drink the grape juice remaining in the unused communion cups. For some reason, the communion bread always tasted better than the same bread that appeared in our everyday lunchbox sandwiches but with the crusts still attached. When my mother was busy after church either counting the collection money or gathering the communion things to be washed, my sister and I would walk across the road to the Bulls' house. It was a huge yellow house with white trim and bright red shutters on every window. Being the residence of a summer family, it was empty at this time of year. There was a wonderful sunlit porch that wrapped around two sides of the house. We played tag there, racing back and forth as fast as we could go, our feet echoing in the empty silence until my mother called us to go home.

All the children living on the island in winter attended Sunday school, and sometimes we would put on plays at special times of the year. One Easter, the girls were all dressed as tulips and daffodils in the costumes my mother had made for us. The skirts were fashioned from crepe paper in a variety of bright colors with the bottoms cut in scalloped points to represent the flower petals. We also wore nylon stockings that were dyed green to look like stems. My biggest concern that Sunday was that Jimmy Patterson's part required him to lie down on the floor. My mother kept telling me to move forward—that I was too far in the back away from the garden of flowers. But I was sure that if I did that, Jimmy Patterson would be looking up my skirt. So I planted my feet where they were and refused to move.

Starting when I was about five, my sister Patsy, our friend Sue Cummins, and I would occasionally sing during the service. "Fairest Lord Jesus" was one of our favorites, and another was "The Old Rugged Cross." They would sing along in the melody, and when we came to the refrain, I would come booming in on one note and in my somewhat deep voice sing, "old rugged cross." Who knew that those four syllables, on one note, bellowed out in a volume way out of proportion to the other two voices, would someday lead to singing alto in the church choir for over forty years?

The ministers on Sunday were divinity students from Brown University, most with a Baptist background. They were sometimes there for a semester or less, and other times they might stay for a year or more. My sister and I preferred it when they had children so we would have playmates for the weekend. You see, the minister had to come over on the last ferry on Saturday afternoon and then stay overnight and through Sunday, returning to the mainland on the only Sunday afternoon ferry. He and his family would stay with various families in the church, each one taking a turn.

The Gausteds came with their two children, Susan and Scott. They were originally from Texas, and we loved to listen to them talk. Mr. Gausted had been in the military as a chaplain, and now he was going back to school. They came to Prudence for a year of Sundays and won our approval. Not only were the parents very kind, but they had children to be our playmates.

Everett and Norma Greene did not have any children, yet we were still happy with their year on Prudence. My sister and I could tell that they really enjoyed children. Norma served as the organist while her husband Everett was the minister. He spent one very late Christmas Eve helping my father put together a dollhouse for me. Then there was Mr. Lemarr ... hmmmm ... not our favorite. He was kind of dry, especially during his sermons, and he didn't seem particularly interested in children. Still, when he stayed with us, it meant a special Sunday dinner, so we tolerated his presence.

Our favorites through all the years were Paul and Lois Chapman. They were friendly and funny, young and newly married. They delighted in their time on Prudence. They didn't have any children, but that was okay because they would play games endlessly with my sister and me. We had two adult playmates whenever it was our turn to host the minister, and I can still see them joining us on the floor for a game of pickup sticks. Somehow, I think we were their favorites, too, because it seems like they stayed with us a little more often than would have been our fair share.

No matter who the minister was, the highlight of the weekend was having something special for Sunday dinner. There was always a wonderful homemade dessert, and sometimes my mother would make whipped cream. She had a metal canister that looked like a big silver bullet. It had two parts, and into one part went fresh cream that she had skimmed off a quart of milk. Milk was not homogenized back then, and the bottle had a deep indentation right where the cream floated on the milk. She had a tiny, long-handled ladle that fit exactly on the narrow part of the bottle, allowing the cream to be easily poured off the milk. She then added some sugar and vanilla to the cream in the canister. The second part of the canister held a small CO_2 cartridge, and she would screw them together and shake it until the cream stopped sloshing around. When she pressed on the nozzle, out would come mounds of the most delicious confection I had ever tasted. This was a much yummier precursor to the present-day Reddi Whip. The other advantage to the ministers' company was that there seemed to be a little less fuss about whether we had to finish our dinner before we could have dessert or even leave the table.

Several of the ministers and their families became lifelong friends with my parents, even after they moved on from Prudence. Christmas cards and letters arrived every year from the Gausteds and the Greenes. The Chapmans lived close enough for me to stay with them several times as I was growing up when my parents were traveling. Paul and Lois shared both happy and sad times with our family. Paul performed the ceremony for my sister's wedding and for mine. In 1979, he traveled from New York to take part in my father's funeral service and to offer the solace of a longtime friend.

— • —

I find a new church home on that Sunday visit. The congregation is small and intimate, supporting and caring for each other like a large loving family. I continue to experience the same sense of peace and comfort that I did in the Prudence Island Community church, so many years ago.

No spot is so dear to my childhood
As the little brown church in the vale.

—"Church in the Wildwood"

Another Mother

Today, I walk up the hill from Judy's house to visit the small fruit and vegetable stand on Broadway. We need greens for tonight's salad, and I want to buy some local island honey for my tea. First, I walk a short distance past the stand and look down the driveway that leads to the former home of Millie and Todd Farnham. I can glimpse their house through the trees, and it appears that little has changed on the outside, except it is now blue instead of brown. I want to walk up the driveway and have my knock answered by Millie's smiling face and warm hug. Millie was another of my island mothers.

—•—

When my mother returned to teaching after my birth, my sister was still too young to go to school. Rather than leave my grandmother with two small children every day, I went to Millie's house. My mom dropped me off on her way to school in the morning and picked me up in the afternoon. With Millie, I always felt safe and loved, and I remember the cozy comfort of her long-ago kitchen.

Millie and Todd didn't have indoor plumbing, but there was a large red hand pump on the edge of the big soapstone sink that delivered icy-cold well water. A black, wood-burning cook stove

31

stood in the front corner, making the kitchen toasty on even the coldest winter mornings. Savory soups and stews fragrant with onions, carrots, parsley, and potatoes—often bubbled on this stove—ready when Todd came home for lunch after a morning working outside. How Todd loved to tease, always with a smile and a twinkle in his eyes. When I got a little older, he would call me "De-BO-rah," which always received the desired, annoyed response: "That's not my name!" I declared indignantly. "My name is Debbie!" His other favorite taunt was to tease me about my dimples. I have no idea why that bothered me or why I didn't want dimples, but I would tell him, "That is not a dimple. It's where a wasp bit me."

The third resident there was a big gray and black German Shepherd named Pal, and we were fast friends from the time I could toddle outside. He watched over me as I played in the snow—I was a bright spot in my red snowsuit. Always affectionate, he was often overly exuberant, knocking me off my unsteady legs. Millie would come out to check on me and hear my irrepressible belly laughs as Pal vigorously washed my face with his tongue.

The only other downstairs room was the living room, which opened off the kitchen opposite the wood stove. The wood floor was covered with a thick, colorful, wool braided rug that Millie had made. An open, railing-less, wooden staircase led from the far end of the living room to the second floor, and a mirror hung on the wall at the foot of the stairs. I was fascinated by my reflection, and when I was old enough to climb a few stairs on my own, I would face the mirror and jabber and make faces, keeping myself amused. Millie told me, years later, that she delighted in watching me, and she would peek around the kitchen doorway trying not to laugh out loud and disrupt my solitary performance. Those stairs were also the background, more than one year, for our annual Christmas card picture. My sister and I would strike a variety of poses on those stairs while my mother's cousin, Mel, snapped one picture after another. My parents chose the one they liked best, and then Mel turned it into a Christmas card.

As I got older and went to school and Millie no longer took care of me during the day, I still enjoyed her company. She would take me to pick blueberries on summer days, and sometimes my grandmother would accompany us. We each had an empty coffee can hanging by a string around our neck. This left two hands free to pick or allowed one to hold down a high branch, almost out of reach, and the other to pick the clusters of small, dark fruit. As each can was filled, it was emptied into a larger, waiting pail. The tiny wild blueberries were intensely flavorful, and my mouth was usually blue from sampling by the time we were finished. I really preferred to pick blackberries, as they filled my pail much faster; however, I knew my grandmother's blueberry pie would be dessert that night, so I kept picking.

Millie was also my cohort in a science project gone awry. I wanted to make a terrarium for school. It was one of the projects listed in my science book, and I thought it sounded quite exciting. I loved anything that related to science and the outdoors. In fact, at that age, when someone asked me what I wanted to be when I grew up, my immediate reply was, "A scientist!"

My grandmother did not share my love for all things creepy and crawly, and the snakes and salamanders I brought into the house to show her were not the least bit welcome. Her usual shrieked response was, "Get that thing out of the house!" Therefore, I sought Millie's help, and she cheerfully agreed. We fashioned a glass box, held together at the seams by thick, white adhesive tape. It even had a tape hinge that allowed the top to lift. We ventured into the woods and dug a variety of small plants, like wild violets, that we thought would be happy in our terrarium. When completed, it created its own moisture, needing water only occasionally. One day, I opened the lid and for some reason, I blew into the terrarium. Imagine my surprise when a shower of minuscule black crickets erupted from its depths. Millie and I had inadvertently chosen to dig a plant nestled on an unseen cricket's nest. I thought it was a wonderful discovery, but my mother did not agree. The terrarium had to go.

The bond I felt with Millie and Todd lingered long after we left the island. I returned during several childhood summers and spent a week with them. Millie and I picked blueberries and made pie together as she told me stories of my much younger days when she took care of me. Todd continued his teasing but never unkind banter, and I basked in their nurturing care.

— • —

They are both gone now, but as I stand at the end of the driveway, I can almost sense their presence, and I feel like I am once again enveloped in the shelter of their guidance and the safety of their snug, inviting kitchen. I turn back to the vegetable stand and choose crisp green lettuce and a golden jar of honey. After placing my money in the honor box, I walk back down the hill to Judy's house.

I Knew
I Could

I am wandering through the children's section of the bookstore looking for a Christmas gift for my two-year-old granddaughter, Evelyn. I look at the shelf above me, and the book I see suddenly seems to jump off the shelf and into my hands. It is *The Little Engine That Could* by Watty Piper, which I vividly remember from my childhood. I didn't even know it was still in print. As I look through the colorful pages, I realize that although I know the general story line, there are details that I have forgotten. I stand with a wide smile as every one of those engines comes to life in my mind, and I remember when I was that Little Engine.

— • —

"I think I can, I think I can, I think I can," I huffed in my most determined voice as I climbed the orange crate mountain, slowly pulling the rest of the train behind me. As I reached the precarious top box, I paused, took a deep breath, and started down the other side, now joyfully proclaiming, "I knew I could, I knew I could, I knew I could!" As all the cars in the train made it safely over the mountain, the school Christmas play drew to a close.

The Prudence Island School had been a haven of budding excitement the past few weeks. It began soon after we came back from Thanksgiving break when my mother announced the title of the school play to be presented at the island's Christmas party. From that time until we performed the play, schoolwork was suspended in the afternoon so we could rehearse for the play. Any students not involved in the rehearsal worked on making ornaments for the Christmas tree as well as decorating the school. There were long paper chains of brightly colored construction paper loops, paper cutouts of Santa, snowflakes, snowmen, candy canes, reindeer, and beautiful angels with circular skirts, cut and pasted so they could stand alone or sit on top of the tree.

My mother would choose a different story each year and adapt it so that as many children as possible would have a part. The number of lines that needed to be learned was usually in direct proportion to the age of the child. The one time that my mother showed a slight leaning toward my sister and me was when it came time to assign the leading role. She knew that we were the only ones whose home rehearsal time she could control. We would know our lines ... "or else!"

My mother was not only the screenwriter, but also the producer, director, set designer, and costume maker—the last with my grandmother's help. Some years, the sets were quite simple; other years, they were elaborate, requiring hours of painstaking work. The plays I remember most clearly are "Hansel and Gretel," "The Night Before Christmas," and "The Little Engine That Could." In fact, I think the last two were performed the same year, maybe because they were both short.

I was Gretel in "Hansel and Gretel," and I was quite pleased with the idea of being able to leave a trail of breadcrumbs as I walked across the stage. My sister spent the weeks leading up to the play practicing her evil, cackling laugh since she was the witch. I can still see my mother's interpretation of the gingerbread cottage. She and my grandmother baked dozens of round sugar cookies and frosted each one in a pastel color of pink, green, yellow, or blue. These were sewn onto two sheets, which were dyed a pale yellow, and were strung at right angles in the front of the church. They made perfect cottage walls.

I didn't have a part in "The Night Before Christmas," but my sister played the father and had to memorize the poem. I think I learned it too, as I heard it repeated so many times. The set was imaginative, if not complicated. The decorated tree became part of the set, along with chairs covered with blankets and placed to resemble beds. There was even a fireplace for Santa's descent down the chimney. Sitting in the corner in the warm glow of lamp light was one of the older boys. Two younger children sat at his feet, and he held a book in his lap. As he began reading the poem, the light over him faded and instead focused on the cast at center stage.

I was very excited about "The Little Engine That Could" because I had the starring role. Again, my mother's ingenuity came into play. Each of the children had a large, open-ended cardboard box suspended from his or her shoulders by wide fabric straps. The outside of each box was painted to represent a different car in the train or engine from the story. I chugged laboriously up the mountain of orange crates, pulling the rest of the train and wondering if the wobbling mountain, along with all the cars, would topple over.

Everyone on the island attended the Christmas party, which was usually held in the Community Church on the west side of the island. The play was presented on the low stage, which had been transformed to suit the script. This is also where the large, freshly cut Christmas tree stood, decorated with all the handmade ornaments. In the back of the church, there would be tables filled with all sorts of Christmas treats, and each family would bring in their specialty to share. I was fascinated by the upside down ice cream cones that Vivian Bains would cover with green frosting to look like Christmas trees. Kay Miranda's Rice Krispie treats were another of my favorites, and I would return to the table for another one, again and again if my mother wasn't watching. One year, when all the adults were distracted, I took Skippy Grant to the far corner of the refreshment table and fed him and myself Rice Krispie treats until the plate was empty or perhaps we were discovered—I'm not sure which ended our gastronomic adventure.

The final highlight of the evening, after the play and some time for treats, was the arrival of Santa Claus. Preceded by the sound of jingling bells, he came into the church with a loud "Ho, ho, ho!" and a bulging sack on his shoulder. The adults of the island worked to make this a magical night for all the children. Each year, several of the mothers would travel to the mainland to buy a special gift for every child on the island. No one was forgotten, and each present had been chosen with a particular child in mind. Santa would sit in front of the tree and take every child in turn on his knee to present the special gifts. I remember the year my gift was a pale blue tea set. I was very fond of tea parties, so it was a perfect gift, and I thought it was the most beautiful tea set ever made. The morning after the party, I brought it into bed with me, examining each piece and having a tea party with Whiskers, our cat, before anyone else in the family was awake.

Once the performance was over, the treats were consumed, Santa had arrived, and the gifts were unwrapped, the enchanted evening closed with the joyous singing of Christmas carols. Then, sleepy children were taken home to wait impatiently for Christmas Eve when Santa would return.

—•—

My memory of being the Little Engine in the Christmas play and saying, "I knew I could, I knew I could!" is as clear as if it happened yesterday, but as I read the book, I notice the book says, "I thought I could. I thought I could." Did my mother change the words for emphasis? Or was I just so relieved that I changed them myself? I decide it doesn't matter. I pay for the book and leave with it tucked securely under my arm. I'm not sure if I bought it for my granddaughter or for myself.

Cookies and Catalogs

The first tray of shortbread cookies is in the oven. As I continue to roll and cut the small flower shapes, their sweet buttery aroma fills the kitchen. The first batch of tender cookies reminds me that Christmas will soon be here, and I am transported back to the kitchen of my childhood on Prudence Island. As I continue baking, I remember the exciting days and events that ushered in those long-ago childhood Christmases.

— • —

"Debbie, it's here! It's here!" My sister Patsy came running in with the brown paper wrapping peeking out between her arms which were wound tightly around it, clutching it to her chest like the very precious treasure we knew it to be. The first herald of Christmas had arrived—the Sears and Roebuck Christmas catalog. We climbed up on the wide tan couch, our short, little legs stretched out straight and touching from toe to hip as we opened the catalog between us, one half on each of our laps. Any squabbles that we might have had that day were forgotten as we journeyed together into the wonderful world of Christmas wishes.

We sat together for hours, pouring over the brightly colored pictures and focusing exclusively on the toy section. The first time through, we slowly turned the pages, earnestly studying all the delights it offered. The second time, we marked every toy we liked on each page. The rules of the Christmas catalog were that you had to pick at least one thing you liked from every page, but sometimes that was a struggle because I really didn't have any desire for an army truck. Then I would get to the pages of dolls, and the first time through, I could say I wanted them all. The next time, I could pick only three, then two, and finally just one per page, but I still wanted every doll in the book. As the days passed, we deliberately turned the pages of the toy section at least eight times, narrowing our choices while our most desired wishes had been circled, starred, underlined, and numbered. There were many pages in that book devoted to toys, so my mother reaped the benefits of numerous quiet hours for Christmas baking, decorating, and wrapping as my sister and I sat enthralled by that Sears and Roebuck catalog.

Lists for Santa came from this book and were quite lengthy and detailed. We wrote our letters and sent them off to Santa. In spite of the fact that we knew we wouldn't get everything on that list, we wanted to pretend that we would. For additional insurance, we were allowed a pre-Christmas trip to the mainland to see Santa. Patsy and I knew that the REAL Santa was at the Outlet Company in Providence, so that is where we wanted to go. I was often quite shy, and one year, I sat on Santa's lap totally tongue-tied. I had carefully planned the list of toys I would request, but the words just wouldn't come out. Finally, Santa leaned in close and said, "I can't hear you."

My matter-of-fact reply was, "That's because I'm not saying anything."

My mother was a wonderful baker, and Christmas cookies were her specialty. Soon after Thanksgiving, she took out her recipes, and our house was filled with the tantalizing smells of Christmas ... spicy snickerdoodles, buttery shortbread, lemony spritz, and the minty chocolate of her special icebox cookies. Each evening, as the big oak table disappeared under racks of cooling cookies, we lingered close by, longing to taste but only allowed to look. Finished cookies were carefully layered with waxed paper in metal cookie tins which were then stored in our unheated pantry until Christmas. Despite our pleas, there was *no sampling* until Christmas Eve. My mother was a stickler about this, and the only samples allowed were the occasional broken or overbaked cookie. My dad was known to wander by the cooling cookies, and now and then, he would bump one off the racks, saying, "Oops! A broken cookie ... I guess we have to eat it!" As my sister and I grew older and more daring, we tried to open the cookie tins for a secret sample. Since the lids on the tins were very tight, it was difficult to do this quietly. My mother, with her finely-tuned "teacher ears," would call out, "Who's in the cookies?" There would be no secret samples that day.

When my mother began her cookie baking and we began practicing for the play at school, I knew that Christmas was truly coming soon. Each day my anticipation and impatience grew until I was so excited that I could hardly breathe. My mother still managed to keep us busy. We had to learn our lines for the play, and I often asked to help with the cookies, even when I was quite small. I climbed on a chair next to my mother and sifted the flour or sprinkled colored sugar on the trays of spritz and shortbread cookies waiting to be baked.

About a week before Christmas, we went into the woods and cut one of the scrub pines that grew on the island. They were never too large because the salty wind that blew all year combined with the sandy soil dwarfed their growth. Still, they were very hardy and always smelled wonderful when we brought them into the house. The long needles filled every room with their piney scent, especially when the strings of lights were turned on and the needles were warmed by their glow.

There was usually a deep covering of snow on the ground, so we bundled up in jackets, scarves, and mittens and headed out into the cold. My dad led the way, breaking a trail through the snow, axe on his shoulder. Sometimes, he would get lost in his mission, forgetting who was following him, and he would speed up his long-legged stride. My sister and I would yell, "Daddy, wait for us!" as we struggled to step in his footprints. However, only jackrabbits could have made the jumps required from one widely spaced footprint to the next. Even my mother, who was only 5'2", worked to keep up. After much deliberation, we would decide on the perfect tree. My dad always chopped it down and dragged it over the snow by the stump, and we put it up that very night. My sister and I would watch in fascination while he strung colored lights on the tree. Our favorites were the bubble lights, and we each chose one that we thought would bubble first.

At last, our patience would be rewarded, and we could help hang the decorations. There was a whole box reserved for us. Some were shaped like fruit, apples, pears, and peaches, the inside stuffed with soft cotton and the outside glistening with tiny sparkles. They were painted in pastel shades of pink and green. We hung them on the lowest branches in case the cat decided to get playful and knock one down. They were also friendly to small and sometimes clumsy fingers. The beautiful glass birds with spiky tails and the frosted glass balls with brightly colored stripes were clipped on and hung by my parents on higher branches. There were always handmade paper angels and colorful paper chains to add a finishing touch. I still have several of those glass birds that I clip on my tree every year. One has lost its tail, but I put it on just the same. The tree that stands in my living room each year is a long-needle white pine, the only kind that says Christmas to me.

Finally, Christmas Eve would arrive, and my sister and I were ready to hang our stockings. We ran upstairs to my parents' bedroom, where we raided my dad's sock drawer. He had gray wool socks that he wore inside his tall rubber boots for bull raking on the bay. They made perfect Christmas stockings, as they were not only long, but also very stretchy. They even had a bright red border around the top. I worried about Santa being able to fill our stockings, as we had no fireplace and thus no chimney for him to slide down. However, my mother told me that he needed only the tiniest space to come in. "Can he come through a crack in the window?" I asked.

"Yes, I do believe he can," was my mom's reply. Since our windows were not very tight, I was easily reassured.

It was a struggle to say goodnight, with anticipation bubbling inside me, making my tummy feel funny and sleep elusive. The first light of day brought my sister and me out of bed and running to our parents' room to beg permission to go downstairs and see what Santa brought us. One year, when we spent Christmas at my aunt and uncle's in New Hampshire, my parents came to bed very late after a Christmas party. Patsy and I woke up, ready to go downstairs, and asked, "Is it time to get up?"

"No!" My mother replied.

"Well, when can we get up?"

"When the stars are gone," was her reply.

I'm sure my mother figured this would allow them a few hours of sleep. My sister was not to be deterred, and of course, I joined in her plan. We got out of bed, pulled down the shades on our windows, and ran out of the bedroom, shouting, "Mommy, Mommy! The stars are gone!" It didn't work.

Our Christmas morning ritual never varied. Stockings were our first priority. They were filled with small but wonderful treasures—games like jacks or Old Maid cards, sweet treats like candy canes or marzipan, and always, tucked in the very bottom of the toe, foil-covered chocolate coins, Hanukkah gelt. Santa also left us each a special gift. Next to my stocking would usually be a new doll, and my sister much preferred to find a new book. One year, Santa left me a dollhouse, and I could hardly contain my excitement. That page in the catalog had been circled, starred, and underlined again and again—Santa had heard my wish.

After stockings, it was time for breakfast, as presents were not opened until breakfast was finished. I'm sure my mother always made something wonderful for Christmas breakfast, but I have no memory of what it was. I can only remember trying to choke down a few bites, and the agony of waiting for the grown-ups to finish eating so that FINALLY we could investigate packages. My mother always used red and green yarn to finish the wrapping and tie the tags. She would attach the tags upside down so there was no way to determine which packages were mine. I never had any desire to know what was *in* the presents ahead of time—but oh, how I yearned to know which ones belonged to me! Once I could read my name, when I thought no one could see, I would tiptoe over to the tree and peek at the tags of the most interesting packages. Then I would torment myself, trying to guess what could be in that size box. One year, there was a big box about three feet high tucked in behind the tree. There was no way I could reach it to look at the tag, but I was convinced it was a doll for me. Imagine my disappointment when it turned out to be a clothes hamper for my sister!

Of course, there were surprises under the tree, but there were also some constants that we eagerly anticipated. Every year, my grandmother gave us a book of assorted Lifesavers and a box of forty-eight Crayola crayons. I can still smell the new crayon smell and taste my favorite butter rum Lifesavers. There was always a game that my sister and I received jointly and played with my parents on long winter evenings. Pirate and Traveler, Game of the States, Go to the Head of the Class, Pickup Sticks—each one brought hours of enjoyment. Some of them are still in my game cupboard, played first with my children and now with my grandchildren.

After I was married and had my own children, my mother told me that it was my dad who always made sure there were toys and games under the tree. She was more apt to choose a practical gift like socks or make us new pajamas. One year, she made us wool bathrobes. Mine was a soft, rust-colored checkered pattern, and it reached all the way to the floor. I could not wear that bathrobe out! It followed me to college, now reaching my knees, still as warm as that Christmas morning when it was under the tree. My dad, on the other hand, built doll bunk beds for my sister and me, and my mother and grandmother made the bedding for the bunk beds, complete with a bolster pillow—they too survived years of enjoyment until I finally traded my dolls for other interests. Another year, Daddy gave me an Erector set. He and I spent hours constructing a Ferris wheel that really turned and even allowed the seats to stay right-side up!

— ● —

Today, on Christmas morning, the long-established ritual continues. First stockings and then breakfast, which includes a homemade treat, usually scones that I have made. Also added are lox and bagels in my dad's memory. Finally, we gather around the tree to open packages. Just as I remember from childhood, the presents are all passed out and then we take turns, starting with the youngest, choosing a package and guessing what we might find before we open it. Only one present is opened at a time so that the anticipation and surprise can be enjoyed by all. Over the years, each of my three boys has had a turn playing Santa and distributing the packages. This year, it is my oldest son Eric with his two boys, Ethan and Owen, who will act as helpers. Still, I don't remember anyone taking more delight, or being filled with more joy, in playing the role of Santa than my Jewish dad, Sol.

I gently layer the last shortbread cookie between pieces of waxed paper and close the tight-fitting lid of the metal tin, just as my mother did so long ago. The memories of those childhood Christmases linger in my mind like the sweet taste of shortbread on my tongue. The advent of Christmas still fills me with joy and anticipation. This year, it isn't Santa's arrival on December 24th that I eagerly await, but that of my three children, their wives, and my grandchildren.

Cats and Dolls I Have Known

I peek out the window, hoping to see a brightening in the sky and a chance to go for a walk, even a drizzly one. The leaden clouds remain unbroken, and the sky continues to pour forth its uninterrupted bounty. I know if I venture out, I will return totally awash, so instead, I curl up with a cup of tea and my favorite writing pad—my

only company on this gray, blustery day. I remember all the days on Prudence Island when my own company was all that was available. Playmates were not abundant on Prudence. There was not a classroom full of students my age to choose from, but just a handful, seen mostly at school. I think about my more constant, as well as my occasional, playmates.

— • —

Sue Cummins was our best friend and closest neighbor, easily within walking distance, and we went back and forth between our two houses with great regularity until her family moved away before the 1954 hurricane. Donna Bains, and occasionally her sister Joy, who lived near Sandy Point, would sometimes come to play with Susie, Pat, and me. JoAnn Morrisey came to live with her grandmother, Mrs. Palmer, the year after the hurricane, and we became good friends. She was just a year younger than I, but we seldom disagreed, maybe because she was always willing to do whatever I suggested. Sometimes, Kathy Grant would come home from school with us, and we would drop her off at her house when we went to Homestead to pick up the mail. She was only in kindergarten, and I was in the fourth grade, but I liked to play with her and pretend I was babysitting.

My sister was, of course, my most available playmate, but there were squabbles between us, and sometimes our interests were not aligned. She always preferred books to dolls, although we both enjoyed playing games and playing with paper dolls. The year she lived on the mainland, she was only home on the weekends. Normally, I didn't think too much about spending time alone—that's just the way island life was, and I accepted it. Then each Sunday afternoon, after seeing my sister Pat off on the ferry, things changed. Solitude, who had been my pleasant playmate and companion, mutated into her disagreeable cousin, Loneliness. I was less accepting of my time alone and sought additional companionship from my mother, grandmother, and a few school friends. Summer brought the return of our swimming pals, but that was a very small portion of the year.

When I was younger, except for those occasions when I ran away to Louise's house, I didn't venture out on my own to find a playmate. Instead, I created my own amusement. There were no computers or video games, and we didn't get a television until after I was five—and even then, we watched it only occasionally. I loved dolls—and babies, too, for that matter—but since there weren't many babies on the island, dolls sufficed. I cared for each one as I imagined I might care for a real baby. They were part of my extended family, and I immersed myself in that make-believe world by talking to them, spanking them when they were naughty, and comforting them when they were sad. I'm sure I was comforting myself on the days I was feeling lonely.

Polly arrived first. She had painted hair that swirled over her head like that of a freshly bathed baby. Her arms and legs were stiffly jointed, and she had eyes that opened and closed, allowing her to go to sleep when I laid her down and wake up when I lifted her out of bed in the morning. Connie had long blonde hair that I could braid or put in a ponytail, a soft snuggly body, and plastic arms and legs from elbows and knees to hands and feet. One year she was sitting under the Christmas tree, dressed in a whole new winter outfit that included a hat, sweater, leggings, and booties. I think it was crocheted by Nana Homan.

My largest doll was named Velma. I named her for my friend Susie, whose first name was really Velma, though no one called her that. My Velma was twenty-six inches tall and had strawberry-blonde hair that curled under on the bottom. Her eyes opened and closed also. Rosebud was my baby doll that I loved to hold and rock. She wasn't soft, but she was shaped like a real baby, fitting right in the crook of my arm. Rosebud was delivered in a nightgown made by my grandmother. It was pink with darker pink roses scattered over it, thus her name. She arrived under the Christmas tree in a bassinet, fashioned by my mother and grandmother from a balsa wood basket and covered with pleated fabric. It even had a covered handle for easy carrying.

My dolls brought hours of pleasure, yet my first memory of them is a painful one, and it is still difficult for me to understand. I was quite young, and I was lying in my crib, looking up at my dad. He held my two favorite stuffed dolls in his hands, and I wanted to sleep with both. He was determined that I choose one or the other. Through my tears, I pleaded for both, but he remained adamant that I could have only one. The more I cried, the angrier he got. I still wonder why. Was there a lesson he wanted me to learn, even at this young age? Was there a painful childhood memory that held him in its grip? I don't know the answer. A few years later, he built doll bunk beds for Christmas so all my dolls would have a place to sleep. I worried that they might be cold on winter nights, so I shifted every one of them into my own bed, leaving about six inches for me to sleep.

I liked taking my dolls for a walk in the carriage, but it wasn't always just dolls that went for a ride. We had a variety of cats through the years, but Whiskers was the most accommodating. When I was particularly bored and wanted something different to do, I would dress Whiskers in my dolls' clothes, complete with a dress and bonnet. Then, I would put her in the carriage, tuck a blanket around her, and take her for a walk down to the end of the driveway and back. She never once scratched me in the process or jumped out of the carriage, but instead, she seemed to accept her fate as my doll companion for the afternoon.

The cats that purred in and out of our lives provided a continuing array of furry companions. Their snuggly warmth and returned affection was sometimes more satisfying than my quiet dolls. The activity of playing with them outside chased away loneliness then, just as digging in my garden does today. Whiskers was a favorite, and she always stretched out in the middle of the paper dolls my sister and I played with on Sunday afternoons. Although wonderful company, she did not necessarily make the wisest decisions. In fact, she gave birth to one litter of kittens in a nail keg full of nails in the cellar. My dad tried repeatedly to move those kittens to a soft, cozy spot—a box lined with blankets—but she would have none of it and took them out of the box and returned them to the nail keg, where they remained until they were ready to run around on their own.

Smokey was one of Whiskers' kittens and was our pet the last few years we were on the island. She was as affectionate as her mother, though I don't think she ever agreed to fill in for my dolls. Sunshine was one of Smokey's kittens—a bright calico that lightened up the landscape until my parents decided we were accumulating too many cats and that some of them would have to go to the Animal Rescue League on the mainland. Two others that met that fate were Midnight and Miss Sniff. Smokey had given birth to them out in the woods, and therefore they were quite bashful and not as willing to play with us as most of our other kittens. It took much coaxing for them to allow us to hold them, even briefly. Miss Sniff was mine. She had white fur with gray and black spots like her grandmother, Whiskers, but hers was fluffy and long. Every time she drank from a bowl, she would inhale the milk or water in her dish and sneeze, thus her name. Midnight was my sister's cat. He was even more skittish than Miss Sniff and would abruptly run away when we wanted to play with him. He was totally black except for a tiny white tuft of fur on his chest.

We had only one dog all my years growing up, and her name was Sonia. She was a beautiful white Samoyed who let me climb all over her. I was very young when she lived with us, and I remember her mostly through pictures. I never knew what finally happened to her, and if my parents knew, they never told us. Regardless, I don't think it was a happy ending. Besides our cats, I liked to play with other wild creatures I might find in the yard. I made pets of various ones through the years—box turtles, walking sticks, toads, and salamanders that crawled up my sleeves seeking a safe, dark home.

I also liked to play games with a ball, even by myself. I would throw it up against the house and recite various chants like, "One, two, three a-larry," as I moved my arms and legs with the motions required by that game. I would make a basket of my arms and let the ball bounce through them numerous times or try to turn around before I caught the ball or throw my leg over it as it bounced. I would play this game even on cold winter days, and it didn't require anyone but me.

My parents and grandmother did read to us and play games with us, but they were not constantly available for our amusement. Long winter nights were sometimes game times, and I remember my dad's lanky frame sprawled on the floor as we played a game of pickup sticks or Michigan Rummy before we went to bed. Usually one of the adults would read to us briefly. One night, after the arrival of television, we watched *The Cisco Kid* right before bedtime. It was an unusually scary program, and I can still see the painting that hung on the wall during that episode. Its eyes seemingly followed anyone in the room as they moved from one side to the other. When it was bedtime, that image of the moving eyes was seared on my brain, and I begged my mother not to send me upstairs to bed. Her solution was to gather my sister and me on her lap and take out the book *Mr. Popper's Penguins*. She read to us for quite a lengthy time that evening, much longer than was our usual bedtime routine. But when at last she said, "It's bedtime," it was the image of penguins sliding down ice-coated stairs, and not those moving eyes, that accompanied me to bed. I learned then that I could find comfort in the imaginary world of a good book.

If I were sick, my grandmother would take time from all her chores that day and play with me, usually after lunch. I had to amuse myself in the morning, so I spent many hours looking through a kaleidoscope and watching the colorful, intricate designs change second by second as I made tiny adjustments with the cardboard tube. I also liked to play with blocks that had been my mother's. Each one-inch, wooden cube was painted with different colors on every side, and I could put them into a flat, square box and make endless designs. After lunch, Grammy would sit down and play a game of Parcheesi or Old Maid—whatever would keep me settled on the couch and not eager to get up and run around. In the evening, when the crankiness of a fever and a day on the couch set in, it was my dad who pulled up a chair next to me and played with me until it was time for bed.

It was not just my sister and I who engaged in solitary activities, but my parents and grandmother did as well since there wasn't any local entertainment, and there were no stores in which to spend an afternoon shopping. My grandmother occupied herself with braiding rugs and crocheting lace doilies and table cloths, two of her favorite pastimes, as she sat in her rocking chair at the end of the sun porch.

My dad often went down to the cellar in the evening to build in his workshop, perhaps making the doll bunk beds, picture frames, or extra cabinets. He could do just about anything. If he was upstairs listening to music on the record player, it would probably be his favorite, Dixieland jazz, and he would sit down with his drums and play along. He also read and read and read. I know he read every single book that is on my bookshelves now—hundreds of them, including *Last of the Mohicans, Tales of the Arabian Nights,* and *Sherlock Holmes.*

My mother was a talented seamstress, and she made almost all the clothes for my sister and me. Sometimes she even put smocking or intricate cross-stitch designs on them. If she wanted to listen to music in the background, it was usually Gilbert and Sullivan operettas. Strains of *The H.M.S. Pinafore* or "The Saints Go Marching In" still hold memories of my parents and quiet evenings on Prudence. The sense of those solitary pastimes that I carry with me is one of peace and satisfaction.

—•—

Solitude joins me for tea this afternoon. Her peaceful, blue presence soothes me as I sip my tea and begin to write. My children and grandchildren have been here visiting for a few days, and now the house is quiet after their morning departure. I get lost for hours in my rainy day musings, and as I leave them behind, I realize my tea has grown cold. And just like those long-ago Sundays when my sister left on the ferry, aching, gray Loneliness has replaced Solitude as my companion. I decide there will be no sunshine or walk today, nor can I work in my garden. But perhaps if I make a nourishing pot of soup, I can coax Solitude to return on this cold, bleak day.

Sleds and Sundays

I awaken this cold Sunday morning to the welcoming smell of brewing coffee and a glistening outside world. The ice storm that came through overnight has coated every tiny twig with ice, and as the sun rises, each one sparkles in the early morning light. Although the sky is now a brilliant blue, I can see a treacherous layer of ice still coating the nearby road. As I sip my coffee and enjoy the winter-painted landscape, I remember a different view, the one from the windows of my childhood home on Prudence Island.

— ● —

Mommy said Jack Frost came last night. "Where is he?" I asked her. "I want to see him!"

"He is very shy, and he only comes at night when we are all sleeping. But if you go look out the window, you will see what he left behind," my mother replied.

I ran to one of the downstairs windows expecting to see my front yard, but instead, I saw a window canvas of intricate patterns—mountains, valleys, and lacy webs—all painted in icy frost. Every window had the same white coating, making the outside world invisible, yet each sparkling design was unique.

I pictured Jack Frost in my mind: he was very skinny, small, and bent. He had a pointed hat and long, crooked fingers. He peeked around a tree before coming to the windows, making sure no one was watching him. Then he painted and painted throughout the night, using his finger to create his own frosty world until dawn sent him on his way.

Snowfall brought the promise of sledding down the hillsides of snow left by the plow. Todd Farnham was the one-man band of the public works department on Prudence. He was the fire chief of the all-volunteer fire department, the police chief of the one-man police force, and he drove the truck to plow the dirt roads when it snowed. He would come down our quarter-mile-long, elbow-shaped driveway and push the snow into a huge, rounded wall at the end. He cleared an area a little wider than the car so there was room to park as well as turn the car around. The resulting open area was surrounded by high, white mounds. My adult mind knows those snow piles were probably not so very high, but in my childish mind, they were enormous!

I saw this as the very best sledding spot. My sister Pat and I would pack snow into any empty holes that might have been left by the plow, creating a smooth sled run. Then we would climb up, dragging one sled behind us. We took turns pushing each other off the top, occasionally losing our balance and going down without the sled. Sometimes we would both sit on the sled, my sister's longer legs giving us a push to fly down the slope. Our snow mountaintop was perhaps three or four feet high, and though only a very short run, it was quite steep for a four- or five-year-old. Over and over, down we would go, our speed carrying us out across the open driveway below.

Although providing hours of fun, sledding by ourselves didn't compare to being pulled on our sleds by our parents. My dad was not often available, but when he was, he would take us for a ride on our wooden sled. The two of us would sit on one sled. I would sit in front, between my sister's outstretched legs, gripping the edges of the sled as she wrapped her arms tightly around me. Daddy would pull us down the driveway or sometimes through the snowy fields. One of my favorite winter treats was to start the morning being pulled on the sled to school, less than a mile away. The dirt roads, though plowed, were still covered by a thick layer of snow that was perfect for sliding sled runners. Since my mother was the teacher, she was the one in charge of pulling Pat and me for these school day excursions. You might think that was a challenging way to begin the day—pulling two little girls each on her own sled to school. But, you see, she wasn't doing the pulling; the car was!

She would tie the sled-pulling ropes to the rear car bumper, one on each end, so we wouldn't collide in the middle. My sister and I, swathed in our warmest winter clothes with only our eyes, cheeks, and noses visible, would lie face down on the sleds, and we would begin the slow journey to school. Corners and bumps were a challenge, and sometimes one or both of us would fall off the sled. Then we would have to run down the road yelling and waving our arms to get my mother's attention. She seldom went far without realizing our predicament and would stop the car so we could catch up and climb back on our sleds. The wheels threw icy spray into our faces, and we would arrive at school with bright red, stinging cheeks. It was the most fun I ever had on a sled, and our jubilant giggles echoed in the cold air, trailing the car down the snow-packed road.

This marvelous winter adventure was reserved for an occasional snowy weekday. Winter Sundays were very different. They had their own gentle rhythm, and we were cocooned in their soft comfort.

The day began with my mother, grandmother, sister, and me all going to church and Sunday school. My dad only went on very special occasions, as he was Jewish. My mother would put dinner in the oven before we left, and we would come home from church with its wonderful fragrance wafting through the kitchen. The smells would tantalize us as we walked through the door—chicken roasting with sage and rosemary, mingled with the scent of my grandmother's homemade bread. We all gathered around the big square oak kitchen table with legs as thick as small tree trunks. We always ate in the kitchen, as the dining room was reserved for holidays and celebrations. Sometimes, if it was a sunny day, we moved dinner to the backyard for a winter picnic.

It was a special treat if it was our turn for the minister to have Sunday dinner at our house. This was one of the few times we would have roast beef, or we might have steak that my dad cooked outside on an open stone fireplace. Steak was a seldom-seen commodity on our table, as was roast beef. Pot roast was a more-frequent visitor, which was fine, except that it always arrived with cooked carrots, which I hated. Of course the pot roast and potatoes quickly disappeared from my plate, and there, sitting and staring at me, would be the cooked carrots. I knew Sunday dinner came with dessert, but there would be no dessert for me unless those carrots disappeared. I would sit and stare at them, trying to will them off my plate. We didn't have a dog I could slip them to, and our cat wasn't particularly interested in cooked carrots either. I would choke them down, trying to bargain with my mother that perhaps I didn't have to eat all the carrots, maybe just one or two. That was not acceptable. All the carrots had to go, or there would be no dessert, and furthermore, I was not allowed to leave the table until every carrot was eaten. Oh me, I dreaded pot roast Sundays.

Sunday afternoon, after the dishes were done, was a special quiet time that is still ingrained in my being, seeping into every pore. My dad would sit on the sun porch in his favorite chair, perhaps watching a sporting event on TV. Tired from a long week of bull raking on the bay, he would fall asleep. My grandmother, sitting in her rocking chair at the other end of the room working on her braided rugs, would soon be asleep, too. My mother, sitting in the living room next to the radio listening to the Longines-Wittnauer classical music program, would follow as well.

My sister and I would sit on the dining room floor, playing with paper dolls and coloring, accompanied by the family cat. We each had a shoebox filled with paper dolls, and we would choose the ones we wanted for that afternoon. We dressed each doll in an outfit and sent them off to an activity, perhaps to work or to a movie. If the dolls' wardrobe included formal attire, they would go to a dance. Then we colored a page in our coloring book to represent the elapsed time. At the end of the designated time, we changed their clothes, sent them somewhere else, and colored again. We played with each set of paper dolls for the time representing a week, and then we would get a new set and begin again. Thus we spent Sunday afternoons, hours at a time, playing with our paper dolls until our tummies began to grumble, signaling that it was time for supper.

Sunday night supper was my favorite meal of the week. We could choose whatever we wanted and then make it for ourselves. From the time my sister and I were about five, we made our own supper. When everyone in the family had prepared their meal, we would all eat it together. In the later years on Prudence, after television had arrived, Sunday supper, and *only* Sunday supper, was eaten in front of the TV, where the whole family gathered to watch Disneyland.

Sundays, my frequent choice for supper was a plate of Ritz crackers, and every cracker was spread with a different topping of whatever I could find in the refrigerator. One cracker for each kind of jelly—including grape, strawberry, and mint—a cracker for Marshmallow Fluff, one for peanut butter, another coated with pimento cheese spread, several for a slice of American cheese cut in quarters—one quarter per cracker—and sometimes I would add a piece or two of pickled herring. I covered a dinner plate with my selections and ate them all, saving my favorite jelly or perhaps the Marshmallow Fluff for last. My sister's supper was usually a salami sandwich.

Occasionally my mom or dad would make a treat for Sunday night supper. Perhaps my mother would make waffles on a cold Sunday evening or maybe scones or popovers, and that would be supper for all of us. My dad's specialty was cheese blintzes, and we would beg him to make them. His were a special variety of blintzes, unlike any you could find in today's restaurants. He made them with Uneeda Biscuits, and he would mix a filling of cottage cheese, sour cream, raisins, cinnamon, and vanilla. This was sandwiched between two crackers that were then dipped into an egg batter like French toast and cooked in a cast iron frying pan. While they were still hot from the skillet, we topped them with a spoonful of powdered sugar, and they were wonderful.

One Sunday afternoon, when it was getting toward suppertime, I went into the kitchen. There was my dad, standing over the big wooden bread board with huge gobs of sticky dough hanging like ribbons from his hands. He had decided to make doughnuts on his own. He turned around and looked at me and said, "I think you better go get your mother." The doughnuts never appeared, but my mother managed to take that sticky, gooey mass and thin it a little more, and we had waffles for supper that night.

— • —

The sun has melted the icy coating from the trees and the road, and I enjoy a long, chilly, afternoon walk. I return to my house, which remains snug and warm thanks to modern windows that don't allow the heat to escape. I must admit, I sometimes miss the intricate icy window paintings of long ago that Jack Frost left behind. When the light begins to fade, I think about Sunday supper. Perhaps I will make waffles and embrace my warm, winter memories.

Bluebirds on Washday

Bluebirds? Bluebirds at my bird feeders? Is that possible? I have lived in Chepachet for over thirty-five years, and in all that time, I have seen only one bluebird in my yard. And yet, here they sit, their chubby, red-breasted roundness, hunched and fluffed against the wind and swirling snow outside my window. Their intense blue backs are unlike any other—they *are* bluebirds, three of them! I am suddenly warmed by the memories they bring of Prudence Island, where bluebirds were plentiful when I was a child. I remember hanging clothes with my grandmother on a warm summer day. Bluebirds

would perch on the clothes post, singing their cheery call, and were a sudden dart of brilliant blue when they flew away. Memories of washday creep in.

—•—

The washing machine lived in the corner of the kitchen, tucked up against the refrigerator and out of the way. On Tuesdays, it was dragged from its normal home to the middle of the kitchen floor. The hoses were connected at the sink—one attached to the faucet to fill the wash tub and one hanging over the edge of the sink for emptying the water. The round cover lifted off completely to reveal the agitator inside, and on the back, above the washtub, was a handle and a set of four rollers for wringing the water from the clothes. A cord stretched to one side of the kitchen where it was plugged into an electrical outlet.

On washday, I would stand next to the washtub watching the clothes and soapy water whirl back and forth in a bubbly froth. My grandmother kept a watchful eye to make sure that no curious fingers found their way into the swirling water. The clothes were fed through the wringer twice: once after they were washed, at which time the soapy water was let out and the tub refilled with fresh water, and once after they were rinsed.

When my grandmother was ready to start the wringing process, she would say, "Time for you to move away so you don't get caught."

Once the clothes were started by turning the handle, the wringer quickly gobbled them up and automatically spit them out the back side of the washer into the waiting wicker basket like large pieces of flattened pasta. The worry of getting caught was very real, as the rollers were not particular about what they consumed—fingers and hands were as tasty to them as just-washed clothes and devoured just as quickly. My fascination with the process often drew me back toward the washing machine, at which point my grandmother would remind me of her encounter with the wringer that ended with a trip by row boat to the doctor on the mainland—and twenty stitches in her hand and arm.

The clothes yard was off to the side of the house in an open field, well away from overhanging trees. Four sturdy posts formed a large rectangle with the clothesline stretched between them. The clothes were hung with the edge of one piece overlapping the next to conserve both space and clothes pins. My job was to hang socks and my father's handkerchiefs while the larger pieces were left to my grandmother. I enjoyed the methodical and orderly process, and even today, if there are clothes to be hung when I visit my friend Judy on Prudence Island, I find it a soothing and relaxing task.

The clotheslines had to be low enough so we could reach them when hanging the clothes, but when the heavy, wet wash was added, they stretched, resulting in some pieces dragging on the ground. The solution was a clothes pole—a long, forked pole that was wedged into the middle of the line to push it up. I liked to hold it and try to run as fast as I could until all the clothes were dancing in the wind, well above the ground. I usually needed a little help.

Warm summer breezes kept the clothes moving and softened them somewhat as they dried. Winter, however, offered much less appeal for hanging clothes. First, hands and fingers would be numb from hanging the cold, wet wash. When it was time to bring in the washing, it was impossible to fold anything as you took it from the line, as the clothes would all be frozen and stiff and could only be stretched across the top of the laundry basket. I hated giving up my undershirts to winter washday because when they came in from the line, they would feel rough and scratchy. It took at least two days of wear to return one to a soft, comfy state. Sometimes I would hide my undershirts so my mother couldn't find them to wash! Still, when it was time for bed, sliding between sheets that wrapped you in the smell of sunshine and fresh air was a treat any time of year.

In 1951, when I was five years old, progress came to Prudence Island in the form of an automatic washing machine. It was totally enclosed by white enamel with no wringer to be found. It arrived one Saturday on the morning ferry, just as my mother left on the same boat to go to Providence for the day. The house had been recently remodeled, and a spot had been saved in the kitchen for this new machine. The pipes were all in place, so my dad was able to finish the job of connecting it. He was so pleased with himself and wanted to surprise my mother by doing laundry while she was gone. I think there was also an element of childish glee—he had a new toy, and he wanted to be the first to use it!

He stood beside the machine, put in some clothes, and dumped in the powdered soap. In my ever-tactful way, I asked, "Daddy, don't you think you should wait until Mommy gets home?"

"Of course not. There's nothing to it," was his gruff reply. And so he turned the dial, and the machine began to make all sorts of interesting noises. We left it to do its magic work.

About twenty minutes later, we returned to find the lid of the machine bobbing on a sea of suds. The surrounding floor was covered as well, and the suds just kept pouring forth. It was "The Sorcerer's Apprentice" come to life. We stood there in stunned but fascinated silence as the suds crept across the kitchen floor at an alarming rate. A six-inch layer carpeted the entire floor before the white foam stopped spewing from the machine. My dad looked down at me a bit sheepishly and said, "I think I used too much soap powder." I never did see him do the laundry again.

—•—

The bluebirds are still there—one on the suet feeder, one on the ground eating the fallen seeds, and one blue puff sitting in the leaf-less lilac bush. They are worth every single snowflake that is falling outside my window in this very long winter.

Emmie
Evelyn

My grandsons are visiting me this week, and although each one usually has his own special time, this summer they are here together. I try to fill the week with activities they will both enjoy like going bowling or to the beach, and I also make their favorite foods—squash soup for Ethan and spinach pie for Owen. We are in the midst of our third game of rummy, and we are about to play Sorry!. The game I now take from the cupboard is the same one I played with my grandmother many years ago. The cards are raggedy on the edges, and the game board is taped together in the middle, but

the four sets of colored wooden playing pieces are complete. As I place the faded pieces on the board, I think of Grammy and the endless games of Sorry! she cheerfully played with me in my childhood home on Prudence Island.

— • —

My grandmother was an artist. Her canvas was fine white cotton thread, her brush a thin metal rod with a tiny hook on one end. From her gnarled, arthritic fingers came intricate patterns of lace, edging for pillowcases, doilies for chairs and end tables, even full-size coverings for the dining room table. The patterns were those she imagined or perhaps something she had seen in a piece of lace. None originated from a book because she could neither follow nor understand written crocheting directions. However, from nothing more than a spool of thread, she would weave a web of beautiful fabric.

What would be your image of a perfect grandmother? If I were to imagine one, it is my grandmother who I would see. Outside she was round and soft with a cozy lap, blueberry eyes, and snowy white hair, but inside dwelled a core as strong as steel. Though many might think her life was one of poverty and deprivation, she built a life of abundance—abundance of friendship, abundance of love, and abundance of inner peace with life as it was.

Emmie Evelyn Greene was born on Block Island, Rhode Island, on February 27, 1876. Her life was not without sorrow, as she outlived two husbands and all her siblings. Her first husband died after being hit by a streetcar in Providence when she was still a young woman with a son to raise. Her second husband, my grandfather, died when she was seventy-one. She lived to be ninety-two. After marrying my grandfather, she lived on Patience Island where, at the time, there were only two houses—my grandparents' and their neighbors', the Bennetts'. My grandfather was the caretaker of the farm there, and it is where she gave birth to my mother in 1914. The family moved to Prudence Island in 1919 when my mother was ready to start school since Prudence had a school and Patience Island did not.

My grandfather again was caretaker for a farm, and he also ran an ice business and a store and built houses for island families. Although his training was that of a stonemason's, he didn't limit himself to building fireplaces but would instead tackle any job asked of him. My mother told me that one day he came home and told my grandmother that he was going to build a house. She said, "How are you going to do that? You've never built a house before!"

His response was, "It's easy. I just have to follow the blueprints."

My grandmother lived with us all my growing-up years until she fell and broke her hip when I was in college. She played endless games of Parcheesi, Chinese checkers, and Sorry! with me, always letting me win when I was first learning. She loved us unconditionally, whether we were naughty or nice, and on many occasions, she offered a refuge from parental anger or nighttime terror. I can remember running into her bedroom on more than one occasion and saying, "Grammy, I had a bad dream!" She would lift up the blanket, move over, and let me crawl in beside her.

Her pancakes were one of my favorite treats, and I would often request them for lunch when I was in kindergarten for only half a day. They were six inches across and rich in flavor and color from the bacon fat used to cook them. She would cover them generously with butter and sugar and cut them into thick, puffy squares. Somehow, it was this last step that made them special, and I would save a butter- and sugar-laden middle square for the last bite.

I can remember coming home from school on a cold winter afternoon to the smell of baking bread. "*Mmmmm, rolls for supper tonight!*" I would think happily to myself. Sometimes the welcoming aroma was her moist and fragrantly spiced gingerbread—with the secret ingredient again being bacon fat. She was also famous for her rhubarb pie. In fact, although my mother was a wonderful cook and baker, it was my grandmother who taught me how to make pies and bread.

My grandmother loved sweets, especially chocolate—not the candy bars like Milky Way that were sold in my dad's store, but the assorted boxes like Candy Cupboard with the calico quilt writing or Whitman's Sampler. The latter provided a little map of the different flavors so you could be sure of your choice. Whenever anyone wanted to give a gift to her, be it for a birthday, Christmas, or just because they came to visit, there would invariably be a box of chocolates. At Christmas, there were always several boxes: one pound, two pounds, sometimes even a five-pound box. She always shared them with us—though if my mother was around, my sister and I were closely monitored.

Often when a box was first opened, she would take me aside and let me choose my favorites. These were put in a special smaller box for later consumption. I usually knew when I would find a nougat or a caramel, my favorites, because they were square or oblong. I was quite picky about the soft centers, and if it wasn't a Whitman's box, the only solution was to stick my little thumb in the bottom to see what was inside. This never seemed to bother my grandmother, and she would wait patiently while I made my thumb-stuck choices.

Although I saw mostly her soft and gentle side, my grandmother had a rebellious streak. Her second husband, Nicholas B. Herlein, was a Catholic man who was born in Sulzthal, Bavaria, Germany, in 1875. He came to this country in 1899 and became a U.S. citizen in 1905. He was definitely not the usual partner choice for a Block Island Baptist girl in the early 1900s. His family disowned him when they were married in 1907, but this did not deter either of my grandparents. I always knew my grandmother loved to laugh, but what I didn't know until recently is that she had a mischievous side. As I unearthed and studied old family pictures, I found many of her in a silly pose or making funny faces at the camera. Sometimes, with eyebrows raised, she would have her tongue stuck into a protruding cheek, a different facet of the decorous grandmother I remember.

Every year, when the summer residents of Prudence Park wanted their Victorian cottages opened and cleaned before their arrival, it was my grandmother who would make them spotless and cob-web-free. She was post mistress on the island for several years as well. The little ell on the side of our house still held the small numbered boxes that had been used, a reminder of years past. These jobs were from a time before I was born, but I do remember her being hired by Mr. Bennett to pick strawberries on his farm at the north end of the island. She also grew her own strawberries, vegetables, and a garden filled with colorful hollyhocks, rambling roses, and bachelor buttons. Her garden extended inside as well, and African violets in shades of pink and purple marched across the shelves beneath the sunroom windows. Perhaps my love of gardening is because of her.

My grandmother helped my mother make almost all our clothes. She had a Singer treadle sewing machine upstairs in a little alcove attached to her bedroom. There she would sew together many of our dresses, shorts, and blouses that had been cut from colorful grain bags. They also made our pajamas—the footed variety with snaps up the front and a trap door in the back. I can still see one or the other of them sitting on our sun porch and using a hammer and an empty wooden spool to pound the gripper-type snaps onto the cloth. She made beautiful quilts as well, with fanciful names like "My Grandmother's Garden" and "Texas Sunrise," and the bed in my guest room is covered by a spread bright with colorful calico butterflies embroidered on a white cotton cloth. My mother had a portable electric machine, but my grandmother only used that old treadle one.

Much of my grandmother's time during the winter was spent braiding rugs. She used solely worn-out cotton clothes, which were cut into long, thin strips, then hung on a wooden braiding rack, sorted by color. The ends of the strips would be sewn together as she braided. She always seemed to know which color to add to make the prettiest pattern in the finished rug. People would often order rugs from her, specifying the desired size, shape, and color. As the braid grew, she wound it into a big ball, and when the braiding was done, the ball slowly diminished as she sewed the rug together by hand. The main part of the rug was braided with nine strands, but the beginning and end were done with just three. The gradual progression from three to nine and back to three was something she instinctively knew because, when completed, the rugs always laid perfectly flat. Those rugs graced my house all my growing up years and even after I was married. I still have a very old and faded one in my kitchen today.

Sometimes, the cold weather and all the rug-braiding caused her fingers to crack. She had homemade remedies for a variety of ailments, but her favorite by far was Griswold's salve. She had a little stick of that salve, resembling a short, stubby cigar, and she would heat the end of it with a lighted match. Just as the salve would be ready to drip, she rubbed it on a piece of clean white cotton cloth. Then she would trim around it, and while it was still hot, she placed the resulting plaster over the crack. The salve dried and made the plaster stick, keeping the air out so the crack would heal. It actually did work, and it was effective in drawing out splinters and infections as well. There have been many winter days when my fingers were cracked from the cold that I wished for a stick of her Griswold's salve.

Grammy's often-repeated sayings became a part of the fabric of my life and guided the person I became. These little phrases were grounded in her strong Baptist faith and her Yankee roots. "Love one another" and "Be kind to each other" were two that she would say to admonish my sister and me whenever we had a disagreement. Then there was "Any job worth doing is worth doing well." There would be no slip-shod chores done under her watch. "That's a lazy man's load," she would say when we tried to hurry the cleanup process by stacking toys to be carried so high that we would drop the whole pile. My friends and family wonder today how I can cook with a frying pan or a pot that has no handle. I know that deep inside me is a voice that whispers, "Use it up, wear it out, make it do, or do without." I seldom feel the need for staying abreast with every changing style or acquiring the latest electronic gadget. This was the way of island life. There was no rush for all things new, and even if the desire was there, the access and money to purchase them were not. You made do with what was, and you were grateful for that.

I can still see my grandmother sitting in her favorite rocking chair, braiding rugs or crocheting. She would take me on her lap and rock me whenever I was sick or upset or just in need of a little snuggling. Sometimes, if she was busy, just rocking in her chair by myself was a source of comfort. When my first baby was born, my parents had her rocking chair refurbished for me, and I rocked all three of my sons in it when they were babies and young children. The last one would crawl onto my lap every night at bedtime until his feet were touching the floor.

— • —

I wonder what my grandchildren will remember about me. Will they remember the games that we played—rummy, Sorry!, soccer, basketball, and the races when they would give me a running start? I hope they remember the cookies I baked, the time they spent helping me in my garden, and their own special week with me each summer. Will they remember the songs I sang to them when I tucked them in? Or the one reserved for the time to go home, "I love you a bushel and a peck, a bushel and a peck, and a hug around the neck?" I hope they know that I love them unconditionally with every fiber of my being, but I also hope they remember the family picture times, when I made funny faces, too.

May Day

The wind is blowing fiercely out of the northwest, and whitecaps frost the steely gray water of the bay. This is not the usual day we choose to open Judy Little's Prudence Island home. As the rain continues, I think of another May Day, long ago, when a cold drizzle hampered our outside activity.

— • —

"Where are they? We have been waiting forever! Why don't they come?" These were the thoughts racing through my seven-year-old mind on a damp and chilly May 1 in 1953.

Spring brought a variety of new adventures to our one-room school house. My mother occasionally took us on walks to identify

local birds and wild-flowers. We picked the flowers and recorded a list of every bird we saw or heard. Then we brought them back to school where we matched them with pictures in bird and wildflower books. My mother had grown up on the island, and she could identify almost any flower we found or bird that we heard. These excursions were always welcome, providing a change from the routine of our day as well as an extended lunch hour recess. Nature walks were often spontaneous and an unexpected treat, but the real highlight of spring was our annual May Day celebration.

The excitement at school had been building as the first day of May approached. We were all making May baskets from brightly colored construction paper. The paper was cut and folded into a variety of basket shapes: square, round, or rectangular, and it was all held together with carefully applied school paste. Cut-out flowers, butterflies, and other designs were pasted on the sides, and finally a paper handle was added to complete the basket. I can still envision my best-loved one. It was pink, my favorite color, and though it started as a rectangle, there were extra folds and cuts so that when finished, the ends of the basket slanted out like a little double-stern boat. I thought it was exceptionally beautiful.

Making May baskets was fun, but the real excitement came when it was time to deliver them on May Day. My mother and grand-mother had been baking cookies and small cakes, and these were tucked into the baskets, along with freshly picked spring flowers from our yard, which included violets, Johnny-jump-ups, daffodils, and grape hyacinths. Each completed basket was unique. All the May baskets were lined up on the back seat of the car, and then my mother, sister, and I traveled around the island to deliver them to various families. As we drove, we planned our escape route and hiding place for the upcoming house. We parked down the road or around the bend from our delivery point and then surreptitiously approached the house. After hanging the basket on the doorknob, we knocked and then ran like escaping bank robbers to our hiding spot. My heart always beat wildly, as the worry of early discovery made speed imperative. I was as quiet as I could be, my whole body wriggling like a puppy with anticipation as we waited for the recipient of the basket to come and find us. Delighted shouts and laughter always accompanied the discovery of our hiding place. We would go back to the house for a short visit, and occasionally cookies, until we were off to the next stop, the suspense building once again.

The damp, spring chill seeped beneath my jacket on May 1, 1953, when we left a basket at the home of the Grant family. We ran to hide in the shelter of a summer house porch, still empty in the early spring. We waited … and waited … and waited. But no one came to find us! My mother finally said, "You girls stay here, and I'll go see if the basket is still on the doorstep."

Alas, the basket was gone, and the door was tightly shut with no sign of anyone out searching for us. My mother knocked on the door and found Mrs. Grant's mother home alone. She was French and was unfamiliar with our Rhode Island May basket custom. She simply opened the door, found the May basket, took it inside, and shut the door!

We bolstered our spirits and offset our disappointment by making our next stop: Louise Chase's house. My mother said she was the best cook on the island, and her kitchen was always fragrant with something yummy baking in the oven of the wood stove. We were never allowed to leave without sampling the treat when it emerged from the oven, hot and delicious. Her Prudence Blueberry Cake was my favorite then and is the recipe I still use today. As we left Mrs. Chase's house, our tummies warmed by generous servings of coffee cake, the sun broke through the spring drizzle and carried us to our last May Basket stop.

These memories returned over the years as May Day approached, and as an adult, I sometimes made a May basket to hang on my parents' door. I still fashioned it from paper and filled it with homemade treats and flowers. Then, after parking my car around the corner, I placed it on my parents' front step. I would quickly run and hide in the secret spot I had planned in advance. My dad was often the one to come search out my hiding place. It was a simple memory rekindled, but he always found me with a smile lighting his face and seldom-seen tears in his eyes.

— • —

Even rainy days on Prudence Island find their own rhythm and satisfaction. Judy and I continue working in tandem, cleaning kitchen cabinet shelves and airing beds. Everything will be ready for the arrival of warm summer days. I have no May Baskets to deliver today, but when I board the ferry in the late afternoon, the sun breaks through the rain and the clouds that have kept us inside all day and continues to shine as I travel home.

Running To Louise's House

"God made rainy days so gardeners can get their housework done." This quote by an unknown author is stuck to my refrigerator. It is very appropriate since sunny spring days entice me to spend most of my time in the garden. I decide to take the quote to heart on this rainy day and spend my time weeding out drawers and closets instead of flower beds. I sort through the bureau drawers, creating a pile of worn-out items to discard, like so many spent flowers. As I empty the last drawer, I find, neatly wrapped in tissue paper, my first

sewing project that I made when I was six. I shake open the small apron, and the memories tumble out along with the wrinkles.

— ● —

"Let's start a first aid club, and I will be the

leader." My sister Pat had just returned from Camp Canonicus, a Baptist camp, where she learned, among other things, to wrap a sprained ankle. She had decided that she, our friend Susie, and I should form a first aid club, and she would teach us all her new knowledge gleaned from her one week at camp. Just about that time, our cat Whiskers had kittens, so she changed her mind and decided that instead of a first aid club, we really should have a kitten club. Conveniently, there were three kittens, and we could each have one. Well, my mother nixed that idea. She thought if we were intent on having a club, we might as well have a productive one, so she suggested that instead of a kitten club, we should form a 4-H club. She had been active in 4-H and had attended college planning to become a 4-H agent. I know she thought its benefits extended far beyond learning practical skills like sewing, cooking, or even first aid; it also offered the opportunity to gain self-confidence, independence, and leadership skills. Since my mother taught school full-time, she recruited Susie's mom, Louise Cummins, to be the leader. Louise was a person dear to my heart, really like a second mother. She had rules that were to be followed, but their enforcement was softened by her southern Texas manner, as that was where she had been raised.

Louise agreed to become the 4-H club leader, and it quickly grew to more than just my sister, Susie, and me. The younger Brayton boys, Charlie and Johnny, and I think Donna Bains joined as well. Being six at the time, I was the youngest member and didn't quite meet the age qualification for 4-H; however, that didn't bother anybody, especially me. Louise had eternal patience, accepting whatever mishap might occur with a sense of humor. One day, she was teaching us how to make fried eggs. Unfortunately, when Johnny Brayton broke his egg, instead of landing in the frying pan, it landed on the floor. Oops—scrambled eggs! Some of the other culinary delights that we made were French toast, tuna fish sandwiches, grilled cheese, and hot cocoa—not the instant variety, but the kind made with baking cocoa. We even learned how to pack a school lunch since everyone carried their lunch to school. We each had a metal box that included a thermos for cold drinks in warm weather and hot soup or cocoa in the winter. We were taught the proper way to wrap a sandwich in wax paper to keep it fresh, placing it in the center of the wax paper square. Two opposite sides were brought together and folded over several times, until it was tightly against the sandwich, and the two ends were then folded in as if wrapping a package and tucked underneath—a perfect lunchbox sandwich.

It was Louise who taught me how to sew on the portable machine set up on a little table in her living room. The boys learned to sew right along with the girls, and we all made aprons from colorful cotton grain bags. Mine had a crisscross pattern of blue curly lines, forming squares on white fabric with a bright red flower in the center of each tiny square. The next time it was cooking day in the 4-H club, we each proudly wore a new apron. At the end of the school year, the county 4-H Achievement Day was held at Henry B. Anthony School in Portsmouth, and the 4-H club attended as a group, leaving on the early morning ferry. Louise, Idene Brayton, and my mother traveled with us.

I remember one of the activities was identifying a variety of cooking utensils, about twenty-five in all. Blue, red, and white ribbons were awarded based on the number of correct answers given. They allowed me to participate, although I was now only seven, still too young for official 4-H status. My mother made the circuit with me since I couldn't spell most of the utensil names, even if I knew what they were. I was disappointed with the receipt of a white ribbon, as I had my eye on the blue. My mother was very encouraging, and she said, "You haven't seen some of those utensils before. You will do better next year." She was right, and just as she was, I was active in 4-H right through high school, even earning a college scholarship for my achievements.

Louise was so much more than my 4-H club leader. She was my safe haven when things were going poorly at home. Perhaps I got in trouble and Mommy yelled at me or I felt like Patsy was picking on me. I would declare, "I'm running away to Louise's house!" This began when I was only three, and I would take off down the driveway as fast as my chubby little legs could carry me, heading to Louise's house, which was about one quarter of a mile away. In my younger days, my mother would get in the car and come after me, but as I got older, going to Louise's house was not unusual. Sometimes I wanted to play with Susie, and sometimes I just wanted to visit Pete and Louise by myself.

Louise and Pete's house was not only the site of our weekly 4-H club meeting, but also the perfect place for the annual island Easter egg hunt. They had a large and intriguing yard, and there was even a fish pond surrounded by smooth, round field stones with clumps of tall grass growing in between. It all provided a variety of hiding places for nestling a handful of brightly colored marshmallow Easter eggs or some jelly beans. They were never encased in anything—no plastic eggs back then—but they were just lying on the ground, sometimes in a clump of grass along the pond, behind a rock, or maybe even in the hollow of a tree.

All the island children joined the fun. We each had our own woven Easter basket, and at the signal, off we would go, trying to be the first to fill our basket. Sometimes I would find a big collection of Easter eggs and think, "*Oh this will almost fill my basket!*" But when I was close enough to reach my hand down to gather the eggs, I would see, sitting on the top egg, a big, black wasp. I'd choose to pass that one by and go look for a safer stash. Occasionally, Pete or Louise would give me a hint of where to look, as my older sister, Susie, and the Brayton boys always managed to fill their baskets much faster.

The hunt was always held in the afternoon on Easter Sunday after church and Easter dinner. If the minister at that time had children, they would join the island children in the event. The afternoon fun continued even when all the eggs had been discovered. We would play games, have a snack, and just enjoy running around the yard as fast as we could. We also jumped rope with two people turning the rope, saying rhymes like, "A my name is Alice, I come from Alabama, and I sell apples," as we jumped.

I'm sure Pete had a big hand in hiding all those Easter eggs (although we all knew the Easter Bunny had delivered them) because he loved children and enjoyed their company. I seldom heard him speak an angry word, but he also loved to tease. Once, when I lost a tooth, he told me if I never put my tongue in that spot, the new tooth that grew in would be made of gold. Of course my immediate reaction was to put my tongue in the empty spot, and he said, "Oh, no gold tooth for you!" He always called me "Peanut," I guess because I was the littlest member of our trio of friends.

Pete and Louise remained friends long after both families had left the island and even after they moved back to their roots in Texas. Years later, my husband and I took a cross-country trip, stopping in a small Texas town to visit the Cummins. As I knocked on the door, I wondered if they would recognize me after twenty years, or if I would feel awkward. I should have known better. Pete answered the door, and without a moment's hesitation, he gave a joyful shout of "Peanut!" and wrapped me in his arms.

— • —

I carefully smooth and re-fold the tiny apron. Perhaps I will save it for two-year-old Evelyn and give it to her when she is ready for her first cooking lesson. I place the apron gently back in the bottom drawer, and although it is tucked safely away for future use, I hold on to the memories that tumbled out of it. They have warmed this rainy spring day.

The Friendly Store

Judy and I have spent the afternoon clamming, enticed by the warming September sun and low tide. After two hours of digging, trying to glean enough clams for supper from the stingy shoreline, we decide a swim is in order. The ladder and railing over the rocks have been removed for winter, so we brace ourselves for the gradual journey, walking into the water from the edge of the rocky shore. The bay is late-September chilly, and each step is a challenge as the

cold water inches up my legs. We both make a final gasping plunge into water that is as invigorating as we knew it would be. We are the only two people swimming today, joined only by the clams having a final drink before we take them home for supper. I don't remember going clamming very often as a child on Prudence, as I think my parents were too busy at my dad's store in the summer to take us. My sister and I often enjoyed being at the store, too, and it is those summer memories that come back to me now.

— • —

"Debbie, Mommy says we can go to the store with her today!" This news, delivered enthusiastically by Pat, meant a diversion in the rhythm of our normal summer day. If we were lucky, it would include a swim and perhaps an ice cream cone as well.

My dad's store was on the east side of the island in a tiny community known as Sandy Point. It was one of two ferry stops and looked out over the island's only lighthouse, which is still located on a sandy spit of land that curves out into Narragansett Bay. My grandfather built the store and ran it until he died in 1947, which is when my father took over for him.

The Friendly Store was a strange and wonderful place for a child to explore. Summer residents could purchase anything they needed to enhance their vacation—from swim flippers to that night's supper, cold cuts for sandwiches, or a rain poncho to foil a summer shower. There were toys like paddle boards with a ball attached by an elastic, snorkel masks, sand pails and shovels, as well as hot dogs and beans for Saturday night or high-quality steaks and roasts for Sunday dinner. The shelves were always well-stocked with a variety of essential canned goods. B&M baked beans and brown bread, Hormel chili, and Del Monte green beans were lined up along with Cheerios, Kellogg's Corn Flakes, and washers for a leaky faucet.

One side of the store was lined with wooden bins that held fresh fruits and vegetables. There were two sets of double screen doors on opposite front corners, and between them was the high wooden counter that held a cash register at each end. I can still hear the squeak-thump that echoed throughout as the doors opened and closed to the flow of customers. The store was permeated with its own special smell—a fragrant mix of bologna, rubber, fresh vegetables, aged wood, and freshly pumped gasoline from the pump outside, all intensified by the heat of the summer sun.

Many summer residents ran a tab at the store and paid for their supplies once a month. However, sometimes money was paid on the spot, which was often a source of puzzlement to me. I saw a ten dollar bill being handed over and then heard my dad count, "Eight, nine, ten," as he handed back the bills for change. All I could think was, "Why is he giving them back all the money he just got?"

On the end of the counter, next to one of the cash registers, there was a big jar holding clam shells. Next to the jar was a glass of water containing one of the clam shells, which had opened to reveal a flower. It floated in the water and seemed to be growing right out of the shell. How I longed to take one of those shells home for myself! However, I knew better than to ask, as they were a frivolous luxury only to be sold. I contented myself by enjoying the floating flowers every time I went to the store.

There was a large recreation hall that my grandfather had built on the back of the store. Sundays and Wednesdays during the summer were movie nights, and folding chairs were neatly lined to fill the hall. The reel-to-reel projector created an ever-widening band of light until, like magic, the images appeared on the screen at the front of the hall.

In the back of the hall, candy bars were displayed behind a glass counter. There was also ice cream to be scooped into cones and hot popcorn to be savored during the movie. My mother sat at a table at the door in the back of the hall, collecting ticket money, while my dad manned the projector. I always started the movie in the front row, licking my ice cream into a frozen point and trying to make it last longer than my sister's. It never did. Invariably, I got impatient and ate mine, and she would continue to enjoy hers with a smug look on her face. By the end of the evening, usually sometime after intermission, I found my way to my mother, climbed on the table next to her, and promptly went to sleep. I'm not sure I ever saw the end of a movie.

Most days during the summer, the rec hall was open and available for rainy-day fun or a break from the hot sun. There was a jukebox in the corner to provide background music if desired. There were also ping-pong tables, two I think, and paddles and balls could be rented for a small fee. Two wooden booths with tables between them offered a spot near the window for customers to look out over the water while enjoying their ice cream. There was a stage at the front of the hall where the local band played for the Fireman's Ball every year. Whenever music was needed for an island event, they happily complied as they all played for the sheer enjoyment of it. The space between the store and the rec hall held a deep-chest freezer, a tiny two-burner stove, and a cabinet maker. My dad hired several of the local teenage girls to work the counter. They would sell candy, make "cabinets"—a wonderful frosty mix of ice cream, milk and flavored syrup—and scoop ice cream from the deep cardboard containers.

My sister and I were occasionally allowed to use our allowance to purchase an ice cream cone. We had become experts on which of the girls working there would give us the biggest scoop of ice cream. Some of them were as exacting with our cones as they were with any other customer. Claire Banahan was our favorite, and we would always try to have a cone when she was working. Not only would she make the scoops extra-large for us, but when an ice cream container was nearing the bottom, she would give us small wooden ice cream spoons to scrape out the last bits. We would sit with the container between us, our arms reaching in almost to our shoulders for that last lick.

We often begged to be allowed to get our feet wet at Sandy Point Beach while my parents were busy in the store. My mother's instructions were always the same, "Only up to your knees, and don't get your clothes wet." We wore bathing suits only when she was on the beach with us and we were officially allowed to swim. Of course we assured her we would only wade up to our knees. Somehow one of us would slip and fall in, getting our clothes totally soaked, and then the other would "slip" too. This led to removal from the beach when my mother checked on us and found us wet way beyond our knees. However, those few minutes of blissful cool water were worth the resulting reprimand.

— • —

This has been a perfect Prudence fall day. Judy and I sit on her front porch in the dwindling light, enjoying the fruits of our labor—steamed clams dipped in melted butter. What could be better? I think about our invigorating swim, possibly the last of this season. Although the swim was brief and the water chillier than those long-ago swims by the store at Sandy Point, it was just as delightful and welcoming as when my sister and I "slipped" and fell into the refreshing, cool water on a hot summer day.

Boat Rides and Bubblegum

The ferry rests quietly this early Sunday morning, patiently waiting for the bustling Sunday passengers to arrive like an empty
stage before the curtain rises. It barely moves on the gentle, rippling
water of Bristol Harbor while its wide sturdy build and open empty
expanse stand ready to be filled with cars and passengers traveling
to Prudence Island. This is a utilitarian boat, able to carry fifteen
or more cars as well as heavy trucks and equipment for building or
well-drilling on the island. It is so unlike the ferry named *Prudence*
of my childhood. This one is designed to be purely functional and

has none of the charm or character of that long-ago ferry. This newer vessel has ample room for cars, so passengers seem almost incidental; there are two very small cabins, painted in shades of gray, with metal benches and windows on only one side. The same side of the ferry is also lined with outside benches, offering limited space between them and the side railing.

— • —

The Prudence ferry I remember was beautiful in a storybook way, like many summer passenger ferries of its time. There were two cabins, one large and one small. The large one was lined with varnished wooden benches and windows on both sides, making the cabin feel bright and airy. If it were a chilly or rainy day and I was confined to the cabin, I liked to hold onto one of the support poles in the center, swinging around in circles and leaning out as far away from it as I could. Unfortunately, this was not deemed appropriate or ladylike behavior by my mother, and I was reprimanded more than once for not wanting to stop and "sit still!" Passengers could also sit on the top deck, a delicious place to be on a warm summer day, refreshed by the salt breeze.

An open area in the bow provided room for cargo, like fifty-gallon oil drums or bottled gas cylinders, and there was also room to transport one car. Car travel to and from the island was limited and had to be coordinated with the tides. The car was driven on board over two wide gangplanks, tire width apart. As I remember, this was best done at mean tide, as high tide meant too steep a climb up to the ferry and low tide meant too steep a descent from the dock down to the boat deck. Taking a car to and from Prudence was not a daily occurrence as it is now. Most year-round residents had an island car and a mainland car, and many summer people did completely without cars while on the island. Our mainland car was housed in a garage that rented out space, about a five- or ten-minute walk up the hill from the dock, I think on Church Street. Trips to the mainland required a walk from the ferry to the garage to retrieve the car and then the reverse of that trip home, no matter what the weather. Everything brought from the mainland was carried on and off the boat, unlike today when you can pack your car, drive it on the ferry, and off again at Prudence.

Today's ferry doesn't pull up to a dock, but it arrives at a landing with an electric-powered ramp that goes up and down, depending on the tide, to align with the boat deck. The boat never needs to turn around, as the bow and the stern are the same, so cars drive on one end in Bristol and off the other end at Prudence. The cars rumble off with a *ba-boom* as they drive over the metal plate connecting the boat to the landing, and it is a speedy process, not the slow, cautious departure demanded by straddling two wide boards. There is only one stop on Prudence Island now, at the community called Homestead on the eastern side of the island. During the summer, the ferry used to also stop at Sandy Point. It, too, is on the eastern side of the island but south of Homestead. We always rode the ferry to Sandy Point, where on Sunday, it sat quietly at the dock all afternoon.

I had two favorite spots to be on the ferry. The first was standing at the stern, where the wake from the boat poured forth beneath it in a churned-up white foam. If it wasn't a cold or rainy day, I would spend the entire trip leaning over the railing staring into the constant bubbles—fascinated, almost hypnotized by the motion. The time passed quickly, as I imagined all sorts of wonderful adventures and enjoyed not having to sit still with my mother. My second favorite spot was in the wheelhouse with Captain Herzog. I would ask my mother if I could go visit him, and she would always answer, "Only if he says it is okay." Then I would climb the stairs to the top deck and knock on the wheelhouse door. Captain Herzog greeted me in his captain's hat with his pipe clenched firmly in his teeth. He seldom turned me away, but instead would lift me up on the high bench that ran across the back of the wheelhouse. I would snuggle into the pillows and tobacco-scented blankets, and we would enjoy a chat, sailing to and from Prudence. I know there were times when he might allow other visitors to hold the wheel under his guidance, but that was never offered to me, nor did I ask. I couldn't see over the top of the wheel anyway, and I was content just visiting with him for the duration of the trip. He also kept a box of dog biscuits on hand for hungry dogs and even curious children. The wheelhouse visits came to an end when Manny Sousa became captain, as he did not welcome visitors as Captain Herzog had.

Our mainland trips were infrequent and were considered special occasions. There was usually some necessity that required the trip, such as a dentist or doctor's appointment, outgrown shoes that needed replacement, my grandmother's desire to visit Mrs. Thomas's store for a new corset, and sometimes in the spring, the purchase of a new Easter outfit. Easter was about the only time we might have a store-bought dress. A spring coat, hat, and gloves were also a part of our new church outfit. Trips were also multipurpose, and Dr. Johnston, the dentist in Warren, would be the first stop. I did not look forward to trips to the dentist, at least not until Dr. Johnston retired and was replaced by Dr. Ramos. I thought Dr. Ramos looked like Perry Como, and since I was in love with Perry Como, dentist trips were then something to happily anticipate. Once our dentist appointments were completed, we drove on to Providence for necessary shopping. There were no highways, and my sister and I amused ourselves by counting the animals we saw along the way. Lunch was usually eaten at Shepherd's Tearoom, where my top choices were a grilled cheese and tomato sandwich or cream cheese on their famous date nut bread. Pat and I always hoped the trip would include a stop at Woolworth's five and dime store for a new book of paper dolls as well.

Our cats had kittens on a regular basis, and according to my parents, we often accumulated too many cats. My dad would have to take the ferry to transport them to the Animal Rescue League on the mainland. One trip was particularly challenging. He had the kittens in a cardboard box that was probably folded together on top. Once onboard the ferry, the kittens managed to poke their noses through a hole in the box or a tiny space in the cardboard flaps and escaped onto the boat deck. I am sure he could never have come home that night and looked us in the eye to tell us he had not safely delivered the kittens as planned. Instead, with the aid of the other ferry passengers, he corralled every one of the tiny, four-legged Houdinis, returned them more securely to the box, and was able to complete his mission.

My trips to the mainland on the ferry were infrequent, but my dad made the trip once a week all summer. He needed to make the rounds of his suppliers to keep the store stocked for summer shoppers. He would leave on the early morning ferry, 8:00 from Bristol, and had to complete his purchases and be back to unload in time for the 3:30 ferry. It was a rare occasion when my sister and I were allowed to tag along. I always knew it would be an adventure, so I was thrilled when I made that special ferry trip, too—but the best part was spending the day with Daddy. I don't remember every stop we made along the way, but I do remember Maxi's delicatessen—I think it might have been in Newport. As you walked through the door, the aromas of salami, bologna, and fresh meat mingled together. This is where my dad bought all his meat, high-quality steaks and chops, and a variety of cold cuts. The plan was always to arrive at lunchtime. I remember Maxi and his wonderful laugh and his somewhat-round belly covered with a white butcher's apron. He would make thick bologna sandwiches smeared with mustard. I wasn't a mustard fan, but somehow at Maxi's, it tasted good. These were accompanied by ice-cold orange or grape True-Ade, and I would reach into a big ice-water-filled cooler to make my choice.

Ice cream came from Kelly's. I think they only sold wholesale, so there were huge cardboard tubs, each filled with a different flavor. This was always the last stop before we headed to the boat, timed carefully so the ice cream wouldn't have too long to stand before it made it back to the freezer on the island. I am guessing it might have been packed in dry ice to ensure its un-melted arrival at the store. Kelly's had wonderful flavors and, of course at the time, it was the most delicious ice cream I had ever tasted. Each year, I would choose a favorite flavor and eat it all summer long. One year it was black raspberry, another year it was pistachio, and another, strawberry, but my all-time favorite was pineapple walnut. It had big chunks of pineapple and walnuts all blended into a deliciously sweet vanilla ice cream. I have never tasted it since. Although they only sold wholesale, they always scooped a dish of ice cream for us when we were with my dad.

My dad was an odd mix. His discipline was stern and often quick-tempered, but he was also the one who would sometimes bend the rules for something fun. Never on a shopping trip with my mother would we have been allowed to chew bubblegum. Even regular gum was handed out in small pieces—one peppermint Chiclet or half a stick of other gum. Otherwise, we were told we looked like cows and not young ladies. My sister and I were quite gleeful as we each chewed vigorously on our big pink wad of Double Bubble, given to us by my dad. As we got in the car, after many attempts to blow a giant bubble, I was finally successful. Then it popped, all over my face, even getting in my curly hair. When Daddy gave us the gum, he said, "Don't tell your mother!" I had gum everywhere, and my dad was *not* happy. He wasn't really upset that the bubble burst all over me or even that it was in my hair. He was worried about having to get me cleaned up before he took me home. Otherwise my mother would know we were chewing bubblegum.

We arrived back at the ferry, shopping complete, before the 3:30 departure. I was bubblegum-free, though I'm not sure how we achieved that besides much scrubbing and perhaps a few snipped bubblegum-coated curls. Daddy carried everything onto the boat with the help of the deckhand, Manny Sousa. I didn't know all the names, but I recognized almost all the faces of the islanders headed back to Prudence with us. Everyone seemed to know my dad and therefore my sister and me as well. Perhaps that is why my parents didn't worry about my sister traveling alone to Bristol for her piano lesson, as there were always many friendly eyes keeping watch over her.

— • —

It is time to board the ferry on this Sunday morning. I watch as fifteen cars are driven aboard and join perhaps a dozen passengers who walk on, laden with their possessions. Unlike that long-ago ferry ride, I don't see a single familiar face until I walk off the boat at Homestead and Judy Little is there to greet me.

Patsy Made Me Do It

I am meandering along the backstreets of Pensacola, Florida. It seems every house has a front porch, and many have added a porch swing, inviting passersby to stop and linger a while. As I continue to walk beneath the spreading branches of the live oaks, I think of what wonderful climbing trees they are. My thoughts go to another place that invites people to stop and linger.

— • —

I remember the maple tree in our front yard on Prudence Island. Its branches reached out, stout and thick, offering good footholds and beckoning us to climb high into its midst. One day, my sister, our friend Susie, and I climbed into that tree. I was only about four, so I needed a boost to reach even the lowest branch. Our mothers, along with other island women, were all in the house meeting with Nettie Simmons, the visiting home demonstration agent. She was giving them a lesson on something practical, perhaps making slipcovers or covering lampshades, and the three of us were outside playing together. Pat and Susie very willingly helped me to climb into the tree; however, once I was up there, they got down and ran off to play by themselves. I was left feeling completely stranded and crying for help. My mother finally heard me and came out to rescue me, comforting hands reaching up to guide me down.

My sister Pat, Patsy in our childhood years, is two-and-a-half years older than I, and like many siblings, she was alternately my best friend and my worst tormenter. It began before I was even born. As my mother's due date approached, the doctors requested that she move to the mainland for the last couple of weeks so there would be no surprises on Prudence. The weeks stretched on, as I was in no hurry to make an appearance. My sister had her own solution, saying, "Daddy, tell Mommy to just come home. Never mind the baby."

There were many afternoons when we spent endless hours playing paper dolls together without any squabbles. However, there were other times when things were not quite as pleasant.

"Here, Debbie, try this. You'll like it!" my sister said, holding out a heaping spoonful of something dark brown. At my hesitation, she said, "It's chocolate. It's good!"

She had said the magic word, "chocolate," so I opened my mouth, and she shoved in the spoon. I suddenly realized this was not the chocolate of chocolate candy; this was a vile, bitter, choking mouthful of chocolate dust, better known as unsweetened baking cocoa. Ugh!

Pat was musically talented, even from a young age. I guess she inherited the music gene from both sides of the family, as all of my dad's brothers and sisters played musical instruments. One brother even went to Juilliard and played the French horn in the

New York Philharmonic. My mother had a beautiful alto voice and sang in college musicals, and her brother had his own band. Pat began taking piano lessons around the time she turned nine. Each Saturday morning, she would head off on the 8:00a.m. ferry, all by herself. I'm sure the first time, either my mom or dad went with her to show her the route to take. She walked up the hill from the ferry to Hope Street to Mr. Yacaletti's house, where she would take her piano lesson. Then there was still a little time before the returning 10:00 departure, so she would walk a block or two to Buffington's drugstore. She would have a cup of hot chocolate in the winter time or maybe a glass of lemonade if the weather was warm. Then she would walk back to the ferry and return home.

Most Saturdays she did this alone, but a few times, as I got a little older, I begged to be able to accompany her. I remember the cold ferry ride, just the two of us, sitting in the cabin of the *Anna M*, the winter ferry. I'm sure she told me stories to keep me occupied or perhaps read me a book. When we got off the ferry, she took my hand, and we walked up the hill to Mr. Yacaletti's. There I waited impatiently while she had her lesson. Once she told me the next stop was for hot chocolate, I decided it was worth the wait. Even on the coldest mornings, we trudged down the street to the welcoming warmth of the drugstore and the tantalizing aroma of freshly brewed coffee and sweet pastry mingled with the smell of newsprint from the Providence Journals stacked by the door. There was a high counter, and it was a challenge for me to climb up on those tall stools. They spun around so easily, my feet dangling in the air. The hot chocolate came in thick, white ceramic cups with big mounds of whipped cream on top. You had to be careful because under that white frothy swirl, the cocoa was very hot, easily burning unsuspecting tongues. My sister was very blasé about her weekly solo trips to Bristol, but to me, it was a wonderful adventure, greatly improved by happy time alone with my big sister.

There were times when we were both in trouble together. My sister claims that my defense was always, "Patsy made me do it."

My argument was always, "Patsy usually DID make me do it!" I remember the night, sitting around the supper table, when neither one of us wanted to drink our milk. My dad left the table for some reason, and while his back was turned, we both stirred a healthy portion of salt into our milk. The meal continued with my dad telling us both to drink our milk. My sister said, "There's something wrong with the milk, Daddy! It tastes funny!"

His response was, "There is nothing wrong with that milk!" To prove his point, he drank from one of the glasses. We could hardly suppress our giggles as he tried not to reveal the shocked expression on his face when he took a big gulp of the very salty milk. I think he mumbled something about the milk being sour after all. In any case, there were no further demands that we drink our milk that night.

We didn't have very many playmates, especially during the months that school was in session. Susie Cummins was our closest friend who also lived year-round on the island. Although her birthday was the day after mine, she was a year older, thus coming between my sister and me in age. The three of us often played together, but there were many times when they, being older, joined forces against me. Sometimes they would dream up questions that had to be answered to earn a turn on the swing. Their answers were always better than mine, and my turn would have to wait. Sometimes they just ran off together, leaving me to play by myself. One day, they said they would play with me, but I had to pass a test first. Louise and Pete, Sue's parents, had not had indoor plumbing installed yet. They told me I had to go into the outhouse and put my hand down the hole, sticking my finger into whatever smelly, slimy mass was below. Did I do it? Of course I did! I didn't want to play by myself! But then I ran crying to Louise when I realized what was smeared all over my finger.

My sister and I shared a bedroom. The walls were brown, unpainted fiberboard, and a curtain hung on the door frame in place of the door. Actually, the only door upstairs was to the bathroom, and all the bedrooms had curtains instead. Like our relationship, that bedroom was the site of some wonderful memories as well as some very unpleasant, even scary ones. From the time I was about four or five, I spearheaded the wasp patrol on summer nights. "Debbie, check to see if there are any wasps," my sister would say, as she was deathly afraid of wasps. Since she was allergic to their stings, I guess that was understandable. I would go in first, check the two windows, climbing on a chair to reach the high one, and move the shades to see if there were any free-flying wasps. When I was younger, I would call for one of our parents to come and kill any offending creatures, but as I got a little older, I dealt with the wasps by myself and declared it safe for her entry.

Our beds were on opposite walls, and each night after we were tucked in, Pat would tell me stories. She made up a fantasy life for all the people who lived on the island. She had a very vivid imagination, and I thought her stories were hysterical. My giggles would bubble out of me in spite of my attempts to be quiet. I knew if we made too much noise, we would get in trouble. She would continue her story, and sure enough, in the midst of my laughter, we would hear from the bottom of the stairs my father's voice. "Okay, you two. Settle down now and go to sleep!" Then she would be quiet for a couple of minutes.

Sometimes she hadn't finished her story yet, so she would keep her voice in a low whisper. Once again I would try to contain my laughter, but in spite of wrapping my arms tightly around myself, my uncontrollable giggles would betray us. We would hear the heavy footsteps of my dad coming up the stairs and then stopping at the curtained door. He would say, "That's enough now. This is your last warning. Go to sleep. I better not have to come up again or else!" We never wanted to experience "or else," so we would whisper goodnight and go to sleep, knowing the story would continue the following night.

Originally there were no closets in the bedroom. My dad built two small, floor-to-ceiling closets of fiberboard, framed with wood. Each one was about two and a half feet square with one rod across to hold hanging clothes. The bottom became the home of shoes, slippers, and extra toys that needed to be put away. The fiberboard door had a small turning latch on the outside. There was no light inside, as the closet was small and not deep enough to lose anything in the back. One day, my sister used some clever guise to entice me inside and then shut and latched the door. Panic on my part was instantaneous, as it was completely dark and there was no inside handle, so there was no way out. My banging and screaming could probably be heard throughout the house. I don't remember who finally opened the door, my sister or my mother, but I just remember the overwhelming relief of daylight and fresh air as my heart continued to pound. I'm sure my sister thought it was a harmless joke and didn't realize I would be terrified to my core. I still hate confined spaces.

We often joined forces in mischief. Every night, before we went to bed, we had to put whatever cat we had at the moment outside. Smokey was smarter than most, and she knew which window above the sun porch roof belonged to us. After depositing her out the back door, we would say our goodnights and go to bed without complaint. My mother would come up after we brushed our teeth to hear our prayers, tuck us in, and sing "Run Along Home." My sister and I hoped Smokey didn't rush her climb and thus abort the plan. After my mother went downstairs, we would wait quietly for the first soft meow, at which point one of us would get out of bed and open the window to let her in. She would snuggle under the blanket in one bed or the other, and we all went happily to sleep. If my parents did discover her, we of course claimed ignorance and said that she must have slipped in unnoticed.

Our lives have taken very different paths, perhaps indicated from the time we were children. She loved books, and I loved dolls. She would sit happily reading while I preferred to take my doll for a walk, make mud pies, or be out in the garden with my grandmother. She was content with stillness, but I wanted activity. Pat would wait patiently next to my mother while Mom made her purchases when on a shopping trip to Providence. I was off and running as soon as my mother let go of my hand. Oddly, as we grew older, she was the outgoing one with a string of boyfriends. I was quiet and shy, especially around boys. She sailed through high school, achieving high grades with little effort. I plodded behind trying to follow in her footsteps, but requiring much more effort for unequal results. She continues to enjoy being a student while I still prefer to be moving.

Through the years, I have been the nurturing one in our relationship, beginning with that first request: "Debbie, check and see if there are any wasps." In later years, she would sometimes say, "Debbie, when I come to visit, would you make me a blueberry pie?" Yet she, in turn, offers comfort to many outside her family in the area where she lives by mentoring, guiding, and supporting those who are struggling.

In the weeks before our mom died, I sat by the hour, holding and stroking her hand. My sister said, "How can you do that? I can't do it."

I replied, "I don't know. I just do."

She thought a moment and said, "I can do it for somebody else. I can do it for someone who is not my family, but I can't do it for my family."

"I can do it for my family," I replied, "but I can't do it for someone else." We are perhaps opposite sides of the same coin.

We lead very different lives, see each other infrequently, and have had opposing opinions through the years. Still, my sister Pat is the only person in the world who has known me since the day

I was born. Inside and out, she has seen me succeed and seen me fail. She has seen me joyful, and she has seen me in terrible pain, as I have seen her in similar situations. My answer is always, "Yes," to her request for support and nurturing because I love her. I know in my heart if I were to call and say, "Pat, I need you," that she would be on the next plane.

— • —

I find my walk has taken me to a small park. The gently moving lawn swing invites me to stop and linger a while. This time, I accept the invitation.

Horseshoe Days

I leave the house quietly for my early morning walk on the west side of Prudence Island, stepping out the screen door, down the porch steps, and into the soft fog. I breathe in its thick moisture and start down the path to the invisible bay; the stillness is ethereal and complete. The birds, normally singing their good-morning songs, are hushed. Even the gentle wash of the water, in and out on the shore, is absent, weighed down by the fog.

As I walk along the dirt road, the only sound is my sneakers crunching on the gravelly surface. The scrunch, scrunch of my feet seems unusually loud, echoing in my ears, as I walk in the moist, enfolding silence. To my left, where the shore joins the bay, is only a dense gray bank. To my right is a low stone wall, its top lined with small white rocks, evenly spaced like the bread crumb trail of Hansel and Gretel, and starkly bright in the murky, sunless morning. I walk for over a mile and occasionally the crunch of my steps is joined by the towhee bird's bright call of "drink-your-tea."

As I turn at the entrance to the Sandy Beach and retrace my route, my only view is the trees lining the road. I round the bend where the trees recede from the beach, and I am suddenly greeted by the water, like an enchanted shade has lifted while my head was turned. I realize I am standing next to the scant, broken remains of the Pavilion, a favorite childhood picnic spot. Now the small sign is the only thing to mark its past. Back then, it was a summer destination, its rock base large enough for a picnic table under a sheltering roof. Four stone pillars supported the roof as well as provided occasional cover for a game of hide and seek.

I close my eyes and hear the sounds of children playing and remember my friend Judy Worcester's birthday party.

— • —

Judy's birthday is July 25, the perfect time for a beach birthday picnic. The children, dressed in shorts, played games while the mothers, in summer skirts, built a stone campfire for roasting hot dogs and marshmallows. When their roasting responsibilities were fulfilled, the long-handled forks were covered with a sticky marshmallow residue. As my sister and Judy were shoving the fork tines in the sand to scour off the stickiness, I came over to investigate. "What are you doing?" I asked.

"Mommy told us to clean the forks in the sand," my sister replied.

That made no sense to my four-year-old brain. "That's not how to clean them!" I declared. "You're just making them dirty!"

I grabbed the half-dozen (non-stainless steel) forks, ran to the edge of the water, and threw them all into the bay. As my sister yelled, "No, Debbie!" my mother came running toward us. I can clearly see her hoisting her skirt and wading into the water, shoes and all, to retrieve the forks.

— • —

I open my eyes to the quiet, empty beach and resume my walk. A little further down the road, I come to the Horseshoe where the water shimmers in the morning light, and the sounds of summers past drift back to my memory.

— • —

Delighted squeals of frisky children echoed as they jumped off the rocks into the chilly bay. Others made the torturous journey into the water, inch by cold inch, by wading from the shore. There were several black tire inner tubes floating on the water and being shared by the children. Their slick, wet heads ducked under and popped up through the inner tubes like little seals.

My mother often worked in the store during the summer, and if we were allowed to go with her, we would swim at Sandy Point and sometimes play with Ann and Cynthia Goff. Summer days when she wasn't working at the store, we would beg to go swimming, even before finishing breakfast. Then we always went to the Horseshoe on the west side, which had been the swimming spot since my mother was a girl on the island. She told us stories of "the Gang," as she called them, who swam together every summer. They even ventured as far as Hope Island, one person taking a row boat for safety. Our swims stayed closer to shore, but we had our own gang of friends who returned every summer. Judy Worcester, her brother Charlie, Susan and Jeffrey Reed, and Stephen Williams were a few of our annual swimming friends. They are part of the same family but a later generation of cousins than those who joined my mother for summer adventures. Stephen held a special allure since his cousin, who was called "Aunt Verena," had a Model A convertible with a rumble seat. I always hoped I would be the one chosen to ride in this special outside spot since it imparted a wonderful sense of freedom. The breezes blew your hair, and it seemed like its own little world, separate from the other passengers.

The huge rocks at the Horseshoe provided places to sit as well as jump into the water, but the curved beach was all stony, not a bit of sand to be found. In fact, we each had a pair of old sneakers, full of holes, really little more than the laces and soles with a bit of fabric holding it all together, that were reserved for swimming. They were a necessity if you wanted to walk into the water from the rough shoreline without feeling every bump and curve of the rocks with each step. At high tide, the water came well over the lower rocks and covered the beach area completely. You could jump off the high rocks, and the water would be over your head. At low tide, if you were going off the rocks, you had to be careful of barnacles as you climbed down to the water since they would slice your foot open, just like a razor blade—another reason for those old sneakers. We tried to time our swimming with high tide, but that was not always possible.

My mother wasn't always available to drive us, so my sister and I often took a shortcut from our house to the west side. There was a narrow, somewhat-overgrown road that led from our driveway out to Broadway. Partway down that road, a footpath branched off to the left. It wound through the woods, past the ice pond, and emerged on the west side by the twin cottages called "North Right and Left" and "South Right and Left." South was where Stephen Williams stayed with his Grandmother Mabel. North was rented by the family of our friend Judy Worcester so that was our first stop. I don't think there were any prior arrangements made for our visits because there was no phone in the cottage. We just showed up and hoped it would be all right if we stayed for a swim. I don't remember ever being sent home, but sometimes we played with Judy at the house until her mother was ready to take us down to the water.

We often stopped along the way to pick up Susan and Jeffrey Reed, who lived down the road with their grandmother, Mrs. Ham. I remember one day after our swim when we went back to the Hams' to play with Susan. I made the mistake of leaving my wet bathing suit on a bedroom floor when I changed my clothes. It didn't take long for Susan's mother, Marsha Reed, to tell me sternly that my carelessness was unacceptable. If I wanted to be invited back, I had better put my wet suit out on the clothesline, where it belonged. Rules were not only for home.

All the children who came to swim here in the summer lived in a much more city-like environment during the winter than I did, as I stayed on the island year round. I remember the day at low tide when someone found a steamer clam in the mud. Several of them dared me to eat it raw. I really didn't have a problem with it, as my dad had often served me raw littlenecks (hardshell clams). It also wasn't a far step from a steamed soft-shell clam to a raw one, at least not in my mind. I took their dare and stripped the clam, dark rubbery neck and all, from its shell. Popping it into my mouth, I chewed the slightly salty, slimy body and swallowed it to the surrounding squeals of "EEWWW" from my companions. I was unfazed and continued on with my afternoon swim.

One day, my mother decided it was time for me to try swimming off the rocks at high tide when the water was over my head since I had been taking swimming lessons with Ann Gill. Pat jumped in first and treaded water while she waited for me. In I went. As soon as the water closed over my head, panic struck, and I reached out to grab the first thing my hands could grasp. I found my sister and tried to clamber on top of her. There was not enough difference in our size to prevent me from pushing her under the surface. Fortunately, my mother was only an arm's length away, and she snatched me off Pat, allowing her head to bob above the water again, gasping for breath. It became a joking family story between us, when Pat would say, "Remember the day you tried to drown me?"

— • —

The Horseshoe looks much the same today as it did then, except the paved walk along the top is a little more crumbled. There is also an added railing and a ladder on the rocks leading into the water, making it possible to swim, even at low tide, relatively unscathed by barnacles. Inner tubes have been replaced by Styrofoam noodles, and there is a raft floating off shore to provide a destination for swimmers. It is still a favorite spot on a hot summer day, and you can still hear the gleeful sounds of children as they jump into the chilly bay.

The last wisp of fog has been burned away, and the bay dances brilliantly in the sun. The birds that earlier were so subdued are now awake and joyfully singing their somewhat-delayed good-morning songs. I continue up the hill to join my friend, Judy Little, for breakfast on her front porch. She now has her own house on Prudence Island, and I am merely an occasional visitor. I think I could still appear unannounced and not be sent home. Just like warm summer days so many years ago, we will wait for high tide this afternoon and then go to the Horseshoe for a swim.

Two Front Steps

It is a warm, sticky summer evening as I stand on the front porch of Judy Little's house on the west side of Prudence Island, looking north up the bay to Providence. The city lights are blurred by a curtain of distant heavy rain, and the evening sky is alight, again and again, with the lightning's shimmering glow. If I choose to, I can turn on the computer and get an hour-by-hour weather forecast for the island, as well as for Providence, which is also clearly under siege. I have no desire to check the weather forecast tonight though. I prefer to watch the faraway storm and let my mind wander to another summer storm. On August 31, 1954, there were no computers to check the weather, and the forecasting was far less sophisticated.

I wonder how my life might have been different if today's technology had been available then.

— ● —

My grandmother stood at the front window watching the tiny peach tree

113

swaying harshly, its branches heavy with ripening fruit. She voiced her worry of losing all the peaches because they would be blown off the tree, and the fragile fruit would be left bruised on the ground. We devised a plan that my sister and I would go retrieve the peaches. We waited for a slight lull in the wind, and then clutching a light, woven wooden basket with a handle across the middle—I think my grandmother actually called it a peach basket—we ventured out. My sister carried the basket in one hand and held my hand with the other as wind gusts nearly took us off our feet. We grabbed onto each other so neither of us would be blown away. We finally made it to the peach tree in spite of the loose wires that were whipping over our heads and the larger trees that creaked and groaned in the wind.

We each kept one hand on the basket and picked all the peaches we could reach from the small tree. We added the ones that had already fallen to the ground and then made our slow way back to the house. Our heads were bent into the oncoming wind, and once more we held each other for ballast. Once we were in the house again, I felt only excitement at having completed this great adventure. I didn't realize we had been in the middle of the second-worst hurricane ever to hit Prudence Island, nor did I have any idea what was taking place on the eastern side of the island.

My dad left the island that morning on the 8:00 ferry for his weekly shopping trip to supply the Friendly Store since Labor Day was approaching and the store would be extra busy. Although there were passing storm warnings, the ferry was able to make the early run. My mother was working at the store as she always did on shopping day, and I think Shirley Goff was with her. My sister and I were home with my grandmother, and at first, it seemed a typical sultry, end-of-summer day. Instead, it was the day that changed my world forever. It was the day that Hurricane Carol stormed across the New England coast on a tidal surge and with a minimum amount of warning, leaving a trail of devastation in her wake.

I remember my mother coming home and saying, "The store is gone." It was something I just couldn't comprehend. Our house sat high in the middle of the southern part of the island, no water in sight, so picturing Sandy Point without the store was impossible for my eight-year-old brain. Still, I could see that she was upset and obviously had been crying, yet her voice was unusually flat. As an adult, I realize she was probably overcome with shock. She and Shirley Goff had watched as the storm intensified. Finally, they decided it was no longer safe to stay at the store and that they should leave. They took the cash from all the registers, locked the doors, and left. My mother moved to higher ground at the Homan's house, and I'm not sure if Shirley went home or with my mother. Mom watched from the elder Homan's enclosed porch as the store was demolished. It took with it a huge part of her life, as the store had been built by her father and was now run by my dad. Years later, she said she was so glad my dad hadn't been there because she knew he would have been in the store trying to save as much as he could. She might have lost him as well, which would have been unbearable. Although the younger Homans' and the Grants' homes were destroyed along with the store, there was thankfully no loss of life on Prudence unlike the 1938 hurricane.

A few days later, my parents were in the kitchen, and my dad's angry voice carried through the house. "Why don't you know whether it was the water or the wind? You stood there and watched! How can you not know what did it?"

My uncle George was there when my parents were arguing. My mother continued to say that she just didn't know whether it was the water or the wind, and my dad became angrier that she didn't. Then I heard my uncle's ever-calm voice—I never heard him to be other than calm—say, "I don't know how anyone could know even standing and watching. The water and waves were rising, and the wind was blowing. How could you know which came first when they were both there destroying at the same time? I don't know how anyone could know, especially when you are being torn apart yourself by the devastation in front of you. You're not thinking about whether it is the wind or the water that came first."

There was a question from the insurance company—a technicality. Apparently it mattered whether the initial destruction was caused by the water or the wind. I didn't know why it mattered—I just knew that the store was gone. To my parents, it made a huge difference of whether there was any money coming to cover the loss or not. I think in the end, it was "or not."

I had no idea at that point how permanently our lives were about to change. It was not just the store that was lost; it was an entire way of life. I was only eight and was able to see the lighter side of some of the immediate challenges. Our chimney had fallen over, but at the moment we really didn't need heat. We lost our power, which meant we had no water, but very soon, my uncle George was able to hook up a generator so we could have power and water again. In the meantime, we got to have our baths in the bay without any bathing suits! In the late afternoon or early evening, we would go to the west side of the island. We didn't go to our usual swimming spot down by the Horseshoe, but instead we went down past the Pavilion. There were no houses there, and it was easy to wade into the water. We took a bar of soap and into the bay we would go while our mother watched from the shore, ready with our towels and pajamas. Although the soap did not get very sudsy in the salt water, it was very daring fun, and I was blissfully unaware of the nagging pain that I'm sure was in the hearts of my parents.

There was also the ongoing supper caper. "This feels like peaches! Let's try this one." Shake, shake, "I really think this is peaches," I repeated. We were in the cellar shaking unlabeled cans, which were lined up on several grayed wooden shelves trying to find dessert for supper. In the days after the storm, islanders helped my parents recover whatever they could from the store. The store had not been washed completely into the bay, but all that remained was a flattened pile of rubble. The canned goods survived the wind and the rain and salt water, but the labels did not. It was a challenge every night to find what we wanted. We took the chosen can upstairs, and handed it over to our mother. She opened the can and discovered Chinese chop suey. Okay, try again. Back we went down the cellar stairs and shook several more cans. My sister declared, "Yes, this one is definitely peaches!"

Back upstairs, we went where Mommy opened the can—Chinese chop suey again. Not what we wanted for dessert! Back to the cellar we went. I shook one. "How about this one, Patsy? I think this is the right one."

"No," she says, discarding it and taking another one. "This is it. This is peaches." Back upstairs and for the third time Mommy found chop suey. Guess what would be on the menu for supper tomorrow night? We all agreed to give it one last try, and then we would give up for tonight. Patsy and I made one more foray to the cellar, shook several cans, and found one we agreed sounded just a little bit different. My mother opened it—hooray! It was peaches, so we could have dessert tonight.

Captain Herzog and Manny Sousa took the ferry out into the bay to ride out the storm. Had it been left at the Bristol dock, it would have been battered and crushed against the pilings in the surge of tide, waves, and wind. Although the ferry was safe, the two docks, one at Homestead and the one at Sandy Point, had both been washed away, as had the Palmers' store at Homestead. There was no place for the ferry to land, although I think it did make the afternoon trip and passengers came ashore in skiffs. My dad's store had been the main source of supply for food for summer islanders, and that was gone. The Coast Guard, or maybe the Red Cross, filled in the gaps by bringing food to us. However, what they brought was number ten cans (perhaps army surplus). Do you know how big a number ten can is? One can serves twenty-five people—not the size you would usually open for tonight's vegetable. When we opened a can of diced carrots, we ate them for a very long time. I didn't know the exact number of servings as a child. I just knew that there seemed to be more cans of diced carrots than anything else. I didn't like fresh cooked carrots, and now I had to face canned carrots—an endless supply. Happily, there were also cans of fudge sauce. I'm sure they didn't come from the Coast Guard, but from my dad's store where it was used for making chocolate cabinets and hot fudge sundaes. He bought it in large cans for the store, and there they were—huge cans with no labels, but with the fudge still intact. It was nice to have something to balance the diced carrots.

I didn't realize at that point, though I'm sure my parents did, that our days on Prudence were numbered. The store had been a primary source of income for my family. I don't know why they chose not to rebuild—perhaps the financial loss was too great. I do know that soon after the hurricane, Ross Bosworth, who owned the *Bristol Phoenix,* a weekly newspaper, offered my dad a job. Mr. Bosworth summered on the island with his family and had known my dad for years. He respected him as a hard working businessman, as a salesman, and most of all as a person and friend. He offered my dad a job at the newspaper, untroubled by the fact that Daddy had no newspaper experience at all. My dad accepted the job, and the changes began.

He found a room in a boarding house in Bristol and stayed there during the week. My sister Pat was nearly the age when she would have to go to a mainland school anyway. The Prudence school went to the eighth grade, and she was going into seventh grade. My parents decided that this would be a good time for her to experience the challenge of a larger school. Our friends Pete and Louise Cummins and their daughter Susie had already moved away from Prudence and were living in Bristol. My sister lived with them during the week and attended Guitaeras Junior High School. She and my dad were only home on the weekends for the next year, traveling back and forth together, home on the last ferry Friday afternoon and back to Bristol on the last ferry Sunday afternoon.

I was used to spending time by myself because on Prudence, that's the way it was. Yes, I had my sister to play with, but if we were in the middle of an argument or if she preferred to read a book, then I played by myself. Somehow it didn't seem as lonely when I knew she was still in the house, even if she wouldn't join me in whatever game I wanted to play. My grandmother's presence continued to be a source of steady comfort, and she often played a game with me in the evenings. I also sought the company of island and school friends when I could, but I spent much more time by myself.

During the winter that my mother, grandmother, and I were alone on the island, we found our own rhythm, unique to the three of us and unlike the weekends when we were five once again. Telephone communication was not as easy then as it is now, and my dad called home only one night a week. Tuesday was the day for our mid-week connection. My mother and I had formed the habit of watching Space Patrol together every Tuesday from 6:00 to 6:30. Once my dad was aware of this, the phone would ring every Tuesday night at exactly 6:30. We both talked to him, and it completed our mid-week, Tuesday-night treat.

My mother and I found special ways to spend time together to help make the long weeks speed by. She was missing her husband and daughter, and I, my daddy and sister. She would pack picnic suppers, and we would take them to the west side of the island. The two of us would sit in the shelter of the big rocks, bundled against the cold damp wind, even when the heavy gray sky seemed to blend into the bay. We sat eating our sandwiches and drinking hot soup or cocoa and had long conversations. We enjoyed each other's company, and the food always tasted extra yummy on our windy perches. Sometimes we would have a special dessert of store-bought cookies that were made in the shape of playing card suits. I can't remember what they were called, but they had a spicy, brown-sugar flavor that seemed the perfect end to our chilly picnic.

Occasionally, we packed a picnic supper to eat at our other favorite spot on the east side of the island. After picking up the mail at Homestead, we drove back to Sandy Point, parked the car, and sat looking out over the water and the remains of the dock that had not yet been rebuilt. Now and then there would be a freighter chugging by, and I loved to hear the sound of the bell buoy out on the bay, mournful yet comforting in its constancy. It rocked on the water, lifting and falling in the swells as it warned boats away from the rocky shoals.

There was an empty spot where the store had stood, and on the hill just above us, the two summer cottages owned by my parents remained intact. Though they were high enough to survive the hurricane, they did not survive my parents' financial loss. At the end of the school year in 1955, those cottages were sold, as was the house I had always called home. Store, cottages, and home—all were gone from my life, as was the community that had surrounded me with love, safety, and acceptance through my first nine years. We moved to Barrington less than ten miles away, but it was a world apart from Prudence Island.

— • —

The dock at Sandy Point has been rebuilt, but the store has not. All that remains are the two cement front steps leading to where the store once stood and a couple of low cement pilings which had provided support for the store. The site of the store is now a grassy area. On the right, toward the shore, is the low sea wall built to keep the water out.

I look south and see the clouds retreating as stars begin to appear. I continue to wonder how technology might have changed the outcome of the hurricane. Would my parents' financial loss have been less? Would they have kept our house and the cottages, allowing my Prudence childhood to continue unbroken? It wouldn't have prevented the store from being washed away, but perhaps my parents would have salvaged more. Then again, my dad might have been on the island instead, and he may have stayed too long in the store. Although the thunder continues to rumble in the North, echoing back over the bay, Prudence is peacefully still, untouched by *this* summer storm.

The Shingled Ell

I have arrived at Prudence Island on the morning ferry. Judy has gone to the mainland, but she has given me a key to her island car. After making several trips from the dock to her car, stowing food for the weekend as well as clothes enough to suit the whim of the changeable late summer weather, I drive slowly to the west side of the island over rutted and bumpy dirt roads, rough from heavy rain the previous night. The day stretches out before me, free of commitments and chores, like the calm blue water of the bay unbroken by boat or wave. Sunshine and island beckon, and after unpacking the car, I set off on a leisurely walk. I am drawn unconsciously toward the house where I grew up.

Set in the middle of the southern end of the island, it was first owned by my grandparents, Nick and Emmie Herlein. They moved here in 1919 when my mother was five. My mom moved back to her childhood home in the early '40s so her husband Sol, my dad, could work at the Navy base during the war.

There are no cars in the driveway, but I knock on the door anyway, lifting the brass knocker that sits in the middle of a shiny varnished wooden door, guarded by two stately lion statues. No one answers. I walk quietly to the edge of the backyard, drinking in what used to be, absorbing the changes but searching for familiar things that might remain. I remember when my parents planted two dogwood trees in the backyard—one pink, one white—as they were my mother's favorite. I watched them work from my bedroom window, frustrated because I was supposed to be in bed but it was still light outside. The white dogwood still stands, but the pink one is gone. Also gone is the imposing lilac bush that stood at the end of the ell, spilling over with fragrant purple blossoms every spring. My memory catches a whiff of the intoxicating aroma on the passing breeze. I wonder if the quince trees still grow in the lower right-hand corner of the yard, blending into the woods. My mother used to make jelly from the painfully sour fruit. I see our winter picnic spot, just behind the house.

— • —

I picture the cement foundation of the icehouse that stood in the southern corner of the backyard. There is a shed there now, but then, it was a favorite spot for my sister and me to play, riding our tricycles on the cement floor around the various protrusions of rusty bolts. One corner was sectioned off by a cement wall that was a good bit taller than we were. It took some ingenuity to scramble over the wall, and our solution was usually a tricycle pulled up next to it so we could step on the seat. After pulling ourselves up and over the top, frequently resulting in scraped knees, we pretended that the cement box formed by the walls was our fort. I realize now, that just as these memories are so vivid to me, I'm sure that when my grandmother looked at the remains of the icehouse, she must have thought of her husband Nick, my grandfather, and the ice business he ran. He cut ice in the winter from the pond in the woods behind our house and packed it in sawdust inside the cement icehouse he built so the ice would last into the summer when he delivered it for the islanders' iceboxes.

A large, weathered, old barn had stood at the south end of the yard, flanked by beautiful stone walls. They were covered in early summer by my grandmother's rambling roses, their fragrant blooms in shades of pink and red all tangled together. As the summer progressed, they were joined by regal hollyhocks and airy bright blue bachelor's buttons, resulting in a confusion of exuberant color. The stone walls still stand, no longer covered with roses, but there is an empty spot where the barn once was.

Our swing set occupied a grassy area in front of the barn on the edge of the lawn. The frame was metal, and two swings hung from the top metal bar, their different heights reflecting the ages of my sister and me, with mine being lower to the ground. The wooden swing seats were hung by chains and attached with large, sturdy screws. I loved to swing, the higher the better, tipping my head back to survey the passing sky, the chain creaking with every downward arc. One day, there were several of us playing on the swings, perhaps our mothers were meeting in the house. I remember pumping my feet to get the swing to go higher when suddenly, as the swing reached its highest point, one of the younger children—I think Johnny Miranda—ran under my swing. My warning shouts were useless, and as the swing came down, the protruding screw grazed Johnny's head, leaving a profusely bleeding cut. I never could understand why I got in trouble—I couldn't stop that swing's descent any more than I could stop the sun from rising!

The small wall behind the driveway that supported my grandmother's hillside strawberry bed is visible, but the strawberry patch is long overgrown. The driveway in front of the house still forms a circle of sandy dirt, but the three-stall, open barn in the center where my parents parked their cars is gone. I can almost see my father's green panel truck coming down the road. My sister and I used to watch for him and then run down the driveway to meet him. The truck had only a driver's seat, but we hopped up inside, one of us standing beside him and one sitting in his lap, to finish the ride down the driveway. Sometimes he let me hold the steering wheel, and I pretended I was driving. The black Chevy my mother drove waited in the shed. There is now a grassy area in place of the shed with a round stone fire pit in the center. My favorite mud pie spot is also covered with grass.

I remember the summer day several years ago when Judy drove me over to visit what I still thought of as "my house." There was no one home on that day either, but there was a construction crew razing the house to build a new one on the same spot. I felt a physical pain in my stomach, like being unexpectedly punched, seeing the house in the process of being dismembered. I guess I thought it would always be there and remain unchanged, like so many island houses. A new house stands there now and yet, as I gaze at it, I realize if I let my imagination take flight and perhaps blur my vision just a little, I can see that the lines of the new house are very much like the one I remember. There is an enclosed sun room on the south side as we had, though ours was built as an addition. There are still three dormers across the north end, but we didn't have a front door where this one is. There was a door from the outside into the sun porch and one to the back ell, which is now an enclosed patio. The weathered gray shingles remained on the ell, even after the rest of the house was covered with some type of gray siding. It held a pantry, general storage, and a playroom, all unheated. I think it was our playroom that was the island post office at one time when my grandmother served as post mistress.

In my mind, I walk through the outside door and up the steps to the left, opening the door leading to the kitchen. I see my mother and grandmother, both wearing flowered aprons, making dinner at the counters to my right. The gas stove, counters, sink, and refrigerator form a U-shape. The double-enameled sink was my favorite spot for winter evening baths. The kitchen stayed warm and cozy from cooking supper and seemed much more appealing than going upstairs to the bathtub. I sat in one sink, feet in the other, trying to convince myself it was as comfortable as I thought it would be.

The large square table stands on the left, and behind that is the door to the steep curving staircase that leads to the second floor. The doorway opposite the outside door leads to the dining room. My grandmother's two china cabinets stand at one end, holding not only dishes, but also intriguing glass and china figurines including a family of tiny turquoise ducks with yellow bills. The mother is only about two inches tall and the three babies, each a half-inch or less.

As a child, I loved to examine the fragile pieces through the glass door, rarely being allowed to hold them. The maple drop-leaf table and six wicker and maple chairs are still in use today, having lived with my son Eric for the past twelve years. I imagine walking through the dining room to reach the living room, located in the front of the house. I remember dark winter evenings before the days of television when my dad showed cartoons for my sister and me on his reel-to-reel projector. Woody Woodpecker was one of my favorites. This was also where we would curl up on the rug and listen to favorite radio programs like *The Lone Ranger* and *Amos and Andy* after our baths.

Major remodeling was completed on our house in 1950, and while it was being done, we lived in one of the summer cottages at Sandy Point owned by my parents. The steep, winding staircase was replaced by a wide and open one, and a wall was removed, allowing a complete circle to be made from the kitchen to the dining room and on to the living room past the staircase to a small hallway leading back to the kitchen. This permitted the aroma of brewing coffee to wend its way up to the second floor and entice my sister and me from our beds. My parents might have friends over for the evening or host the PTA or a church meeting, and the fragrance of coffee was the signal that refreshments were about to be served. We would stand at the top of the stairs and call, as one voice, "Mommy, we're hungry!"

She would ask, "Would you like to come down and have dessert?"

Of course the answer was a resounding "Yes!" and we came downstairs in our pajamas to sample whatever treat my mother had made.

I see myself walk up the new staircase into the wide-open hallway. My dad's big roll-top desk just fits in the corner. I peek into the curtained room ahead on the right, inhaling the soft, sweet fragrance that always seemed to surround my mother. The beautifully crafted maple bedroom set, purchased by my parents in 1942 for $179, fills most of the room. The original quality is still apparent in my guest room today. Two pictures hang above the bed, both in shades of muted gray-green. One is a girl kneeling, looking at a bird above her head; the other is a shepherd, watching over his flock. They hung over my mother's bed as long as she lived, and now they hang over mine. Pat and I share the room on the left. Two twin beds reside on opposite walls, and close to mine are the doll bunk beds made by my dad.

Turning left down the hall, I pass the bathroom on my way to the front of the house and my grandmother's room. It is the largest of the three bedrooms and includes a small cubby room where she could sit at her treadle sewing machine. The bed is covered with a bedspread with patchwork yellow and green fleur-de-lis, and matching bureau scarves cover the two bureaus, all made by her. Her favorite Cashmere Bouquet talcum powder floats in the air, and I know she will offer a safe haven from any scary nightmares.

Downstairs once more, I explore the addition—an enclosed sun porch on the south end, running the whole width of the house. A large picture window at either end fills the room with light, and windows and low bookshelves run along the outside wall. The bookcase shelves are filled with my dad's books, and the tops are lined with my grandmother's African violets. A new outside door stands in the middle, as the old one is now the open doorway leading from the house to the sun porch. The original outside windows serve as part of the wall between the living room, dining room, and sun porch. It was the perfect spot for secretly watching television, installed on the porch, when we were supposed to be in bed. My sister and I would sneak down the stairs under the cover of darkness, our slippers whispering softly, and sit in the dining room, our faces just above the window sills. It was sometimes hard to hear the sound, but the picture was clear and easy to see. I'm sure my parents knew we were there, even though we were convinced we were invisible.

My meanderings bring me back to the outside door, opening on the ell. I pass the pantry on my left and continue down the hall to the playroom. Outside the playroom door is a small passageway where my mother's steamer trunk is stored. It holds an endless supply of treasures to explore and fabric to be used for creating Halloween costumes. Red and white stripes for a clown, lavender drapes transformed into a princess dress, and black material destined to be a witch's cape. I peek into the playroom, which is the perfect place to keep my doll carriage. There is a child-sized red wooden table and two chairs—one is a red rocking chair, the other a brightly painted, wooden straight chair with a woven seat. The latter now sits in front of my fireplace, somewhat faded, but still quite sturdy. One end of the room holds high, wide shelves built by my father for toy storage, but my sister and I prefer to use them for climbing so the toys lie scattered on the floor. I step back outside the playroom door where I experienced my first kiss.

Brad Homan and his brother David came to our house to play one day. I'm not sure why since this was an unusual occurrence. I had an enormous crush on Brad. He was the second love of my life, the first being Perry Como. I started a scrapbook with pictures of Perry, though I had only found one to paste on the pages, but here was Brad, walking through the door, and I decided I really would like to kiss him. Without considering how he might feel about this—I think I was six or seven and he was eleven or twelve—I impulsively devised a plan. I found a sheer curtain in the steamer trunk and hid in the passageway outside the playroom door. When he came around the corner from the outside ell door, I jumped up, threw the curtain over his head, and kissed him through the curtain! I don't remember him being angry, but he was certainly momentarily speechless.

—•—

The laughter ignited by this memory startles me back to the present moment. I am standing under the maple tree that once held me captive. I wonder now what the new house interior looks like today. Perhaps it is best not to know, as some memories are happier left safely wrapped. I tuck mine securely away and continue my walk back down the driveway. The surface, thickly covered with sand, and the elbow bend remain unchanged.

Judy and I have switched roles today, as I arrived on the morning ferry by myself and she returns this afternoon. Now it is I who will meet her. As I make the short drive, the car follows my automatic lead, turning down the hill to Sandy Point. I park and get out, walk to the end of the dock, and immerse myself in this familiar view of the bay. Before I continue on to Homestead, I climb the two steps that once led to the front door of the Friendly Store. As I stand on the top step, suddenly, unbidden and without warning, tears begin to run down my cheeks. I am surprised, as I wasn't feeling sad. My mind and my body must be grieving unconsciously. These are tears I have never shed—not for sixty years. I get back in the car with peace in my heart—a peace that I didn't even know I was missing.

Island Tapestry 1

Judy and I are sitting on the front porch, lingering over the johnny-cakes she has made for breakfast and drinking in the cobalt blue of Narragansett Bay. We enjoy a second cup of coffee as we talk of things present and past. Time on Prudence seems unconnected to the hands of the clock; it evaporates as life proceeds at a meandering pace. The warm, fragrant johnnycakes, drizzled with maple syrup, awaken thoughts about my grandmother. She also made them, unleavened griddle cakes made from scalded white cornmeal and cooked in a hot skillet.

Gram cooked hers in bacon fat, which was saved in a coffee can every time we had bacon. When it was time to make johnnycakes,

out would come the heavy, black cast-iron skillet and in would go a generous portion of bacon fat. As the quarter inch of hot fat began to sizzle and pop, thick mounds of batter, resembling mashed potatoes, were spooned in. There they would stay for six minutes before they were turned. Just before flipping them, she would take a clothes pin wrapped with a clean rag, dip it in the bacon fat, and add a dollop to the top of each one. The finished johnnycakes were crispy and brown on the outside and creamy-smooth in the middle. Swimming in maple syrup, they were a delectable treat.

Fueled by johnnycakes and memories of my grandmother, I decide to ride my bike around the island, connecting to past memories and enjoying the summer day. I ride past the driveway on the right that leads to my old house and past the one on the left that leads to the Cummins' house. My favorite route between those two was a path through the fields. This took me past the Lathrops' home where Mrs. Lathrop and her grown daughter Grace lived in a small, two-story, gray-green shingled house. I think there were two rooms downstairs and one or two stacked on top upstairs. The kitchen was sparsely furnished with a drop-leaf table and two or three chairs against the inside wall. The opposite wall held a large, white, enameled sink with a hand pump at the end and a black wood-burning stove for cooking. There was no flush toilet, so an outhouse stood off to the side in the field.

I always enjoyed going to visit them, but I must confess I had an ulterior motive for these visits. As we sat and had our chat, I would look up at the open, wooden shelves high above my head. Invariably, my eyes would land longingly on the glass canning jar holding the light blue package of Black Jack gum—my favorite. I seldom was allowed to chew this at home, as my mother preferred peppermint Chiclets. As we talked, I would somehow guide the conversation so I could mention that I had not had Black Jack gum in a very long time. Of course, one of them would always say, "Oh! Would you like a piece?"

"Why, yes, thank you. I would!" was my polite reply. All that remains of the house today is the foundation and the base of the chimney, slightly off-center, in the crumbling stone.

I pedal past the entrance to Farnham Farm, now the site of many Prudence Conservancy and other island events. Even back then, it was a gathering spot for many occasions like the annual summer clam bake. Empty fifty-gallon drums were filled in the bottom with rocks and a fire was built. When the flames burned out, the hot rocks were covered with seaweed to create steam. Potatoes, fish, fresh sweet corn, sausages, and clams were all layered in the proper order, based on their cooking times. Islanders sat at the long tables, enjoying each other's company while waiting for the bake to be ready.

Another memorable event was the day that a small piper cub airplane landed in the field and took people for a ride, one or two at a time. I wore my best blue-and-white-striped dress for this momentous occasion. I went up in the plane, safely held on my father's lap, as I marveled at this airborne perspective of the island.

Although Millie Farnham was the one who usually cared for me while my mother worked, I remember a few occasions when Mary Farnham filled in. She was married to Todd's brother Harris, and they lived on the farm. Mary was pleasant but not the warm, comforting presence I had found in Millie, and I was afraid of Harris. He was so tall, from my child's view, and quite gruff. Although Todd teased me on every visit, his manner was always gentle and kind. I remember when our brown box wall phone with the crank handle and trumpet mouthpiece was retired for a black hand-held model. We had party lines, and Mary and Harris were on the same line as we were. A different number of rings signaled which party should answer the phone. My sister and I used to try, secretly, to listen in on Mary's phone calls. No matter how carefully we picked up the receiver, she always seemed to know we were there. Before even saying hello, she would yell, "Patsy and Debbie, get off the phone!"

The Ferry Home

As I ride down the road leading to the old Navy base, I hear a peacock screeching in the distance. This was not a sound I ever heard on Prudence Island in the 1950s, as there was nothing as exotic as peacocks on the island back then. The concrete road on the base seems unchanged, but there is no longer a gate or a guardhouse where you check in when entering. I ride past the two houses that served as married officers' quarters. They are unchanged, except I think they shrank over the years, like sweaters washed in too-hot water. I remember them as huge, almost palatial, but now they look quite ordinary. Still the same is the one-floor, ranch-style house with the two matching ends extending forward in front of the house.

I can remember coming here to play with Louise and Brenda Freeman and enjoying their heated playroom right next to the back door. Louise was two years older than I, and Brenda, two years younger. They lived on the island the year my sister was on the mainland, so their friendship filled an empty place in my life. Most of the time, the three of us could play happily for hours. There were large portions of the base that were woods, and they knew all the best spots to explore. We armed ourselves with canned potato sticks for a snack and then set off on our adventures. There was also a place that had red clay soil, so unlike the familiar sandy soil of much of the island. We would dig up the red dirt, add some water, and make it into the right consistency for modeling clay. After rolling it into long, snakelike pieces, we formed it into tiny pots, leaving them to dry in the sun for our next visit.

Louise and Brenda's grandmother had come for an extended visit since their mom was pregnant, and it was almost time for the baby to arrive. A resident grandmother is almost always a soothing presence, and she also made us special after-school snacks like wonderful apricot turnovers, which she fried and sprinkled with powdered sugar. They were unlike anything I had ever tasted at home. Sometimes, Brenda and Louise would invite me to stay for supper and go to the movies, which were shown regularly on the base for the servicemen and resident family members. Being allowed to join them was a special treat, but one night it had a less-than-happy ending. The movie showing was *War of the Worlds,* and I found it terrifying. I had nightmares for weeks following that movie, and I am still not a big fan of scary movies.

I ride all the way to the dock on the base where there is now an open grassy area, a beach for swimming, and an education center. During the war, this deep-water dock provided a place for United States Navy ships to come and unload ammunition to be stored in the hidden bunkers on the island. It was probably still a restricted area when I was a child, as I never remember coming here with Louise and Brenda.

Two sailboats slide by on the calm water, their sales furled in the still morning air. I continue my ride back the way I came, turning right when I reach the school house.

Island
Tapestry 2

I turn right on Broadway and ride past the schoolhouse, wondering to myself, *"Was the front yard always so small?"* The hand pump that provided fresh water is gone. The front yard now holds two gardens, both bursting with vegetables and colorful flowers—one close to the road and one nestled in the shelter of the addition. I remember playing red rover and giant steps in the front yard, and it seemed like we had an endless space to run. What happened to it?

I pedal on down Broadway, passing the wide mown path that now forms the Heritage Trail. Once, it was a narrow dirt road

that cut across the top of the island and ended at Chase's farm, barely wide enough for one car. I remember the spring day when we were late heading home, so my mother decided to take this shortcut road. Unfortunately,

137

it was not a reliable route in the spring, and we got stuck in deep ruts of mud. There were no cell phones then to call for help. I think we must have walked the rest of the way home while the car sat waiting to be towed out by my dad.

As I come over the brow of the hill, the chameleon bay, a soft, gray-blue this morning, peeks out before me. If I continue straight down the hill, I will be in Bristol Colony, a cluster of summer homes so-named because most of the people who originally owned them lived in Bristol during the winter months. In my childhood, my family's primary reason for visiting that little community was Dewitt's Bakery, which was the first driveway on the right as you headed down the hill. It was open only during the summer. My mind walks through the door of that little blue-and-white building and inhales the heady aroma of spicy and sweet mingling together. My grandmother and mother were both perfectly good bakers, so most of our pies, cookies, and cakes were made by them. However, there was something about Mr. Dewitt's hermits and sugar cookies that were special.

Often, driving home from the store, I would beg my mother to take a detour down the hill and stop at the bakery. "Can we please go to Mr. Dewitt's?"

"Not today," was her usual response. Now and then she would give in, and we would emerge from the bakery, clutching three fragrant white bags. One held fat and spicy hermits, a soft molasses bar cookie that was cut in three-inch squares, succulent and moist with raisins. The second bag held big, round, thick sugar cookies sprinkled with sparkling, crunchy, coarse sugar, the sweet vanilla scent escaping when I peeked in the bag. I never could decide which one I liked the best, but the third bag held my grandmother's favorite, Mr. DeWitt's cruller doughnuts, which was one treat we never made at home.

I suddenly remember another occasion for visiting Bristol Colony. One winter, the Community Church was trying to raise money for needed improvements. My sister and I struck a business deal with my dad for our contribution. We bought candy bars from him at wholesale cost and then we would travel around the island, my mother providing transportation, and sell the candy to residents at retail prices. They had candy delivered to their door when the store was not open, and we donated the profits to the church.

Memories of our business venture spark the memory of Milly and Bud Cochran, who rented the cottage owned by Mr. and Mrs. Dewitt. Bud was stationed at the Navy base on the island, and he was a fine craftsman as well, building a beautiful wooden altar for the church. Milly was one of our best customers, though she never ate any candy. She always greeted us at the door in a lovely négligée, and after determining our favorite candies, she would buy those particular kinds. She paid us and then took the candy and gave it back to my sister and me with a smile, telling us to enjoy it ourselves. We thought it was a great system, but my mother finally said we couldn't keep selling the candy and then taking it back to eat.

I turn left before Bristol Colony and head toward Sandy Point. As I ride along the road, the bay peeks briefly through the trees on my right and then disappears again. Just like my memories, the view of the bay is sometimes a fleeting glimmer and sometimes a lingering presence to be embraced and savored as I bike. I pass the site of Joe Gillette's junk yard where, back then, worn-out cars were put out to pasture until they rusted into the ground. The old cars are gone now, and a lovely house stands in their place.

Finally, as I descend the hill to Sandy Point, the view of the bay is complete, and it follows me all along the east side of the island. I come down the hill past Mrs. Rice's cottage. She occasionally baby-sat for my sister and me if my grandmother was on the mainland visiting her sister. Her house was built on a hillside, and the door was about ten or twelve steps off the ground. The painful memory of jumping off the top step floats by. My knees came up under my chin, banging my teeth shut with my tongue in between. Ouch!

Happier memories accompany me as I continue my ride down the hill. I see Mrs. Tarr's house on a high bank to the left where we would roll from her front door, across the grass, and to the edge of the bank above the road. We did it over and over again until the grass stains were embedded in our clothes and our heads were dizzy with the spinning.

I coast down the steep, short hill to the right, leading to the Sandy Point dock and beach. This is also where my dad's store stood before the 1954 hurricane. Now, only the front steps remain. The beach, curving out to the lighthouse, was the usual spot where we swam when not on the west side of the island. Often we were here when my mother was working in the store. The dock is now posted with two signs: "Only active docking," and "No unattended vehicles."

Back then, the rules were not so rigid. The ferry would lay over there on summer Sunday afternoons until it was time for the last trip to Bristol. Small fishing and pleasure boats also pulled up to the dock on many Sunday afternoons. At the top of the hill still sits the small rental cottage once owned by my parents. Originally there were two, but one has been replaced by a larger building. The one remaining was rented by the MacEntee family every summer, and my sister and I sometimes played with their children. The cottage looks much the same—the outside is still gray shingles—but the windows have been replaced, and what was once just a screen porch is now enclosed. We stayed there one fall when our house was being remodeled. At that time, the bathroom was very small, and I think the shower was outside. That was fine for a summer cottage, but it became a little challenging as the weather got cooler, so my sister and I took our baths in the kitchen sink. Television came to the island while we were there, and Pat and I would walk up the street a few houses to the Bains' house. There, we watched *Time for Beanie* and *Howdy Doody* with Donna Bains, returning at dusk, just in time for supper.

Before I head up the hill, I look over at the huge rocks along the shore running south from Sandy Point. Ann Goff and I climbed them one summer afternoon, paralleling the road, all the way to the top of the hill. We finally joined the road once more at her Aunt Annie's house and then proceeded to her house to play. I had only told my mother that I was going to Ann's house, neglecting to mention our chosen route, as I knew she would not approve.

I ride back up the hill and turn right, continuing my northern route, passing the home of Nana and Grampa Homan. This was one of my favorite stops when we made our winter ferry run to pick up the mail at Homestead. Their dark red cottage stood on the hill, rising above the Sandy Point Lighthouse. My mother would drop me off as she went on to Homestead. I would chat with them, play with their Scottish terrier, and often have cookies and milk as a snack. The Homans were longtime friends of my grandmother, attending all her birthday parties; they even joined us for Thanksgiving dinner on several occasions. I thought of them as an extra set of grandparents, and they always welcomed me warmly, even though my visits were usually unannounced.

I travel past the old hotel. Back then it was white with a red roof, and it was another favorite visiting spot. Marian Reed, whose husband Bob was stationed at the Navy base on the island, lived there with her baby girl. I loved babies, and I would visit with Marion, hold the baby if she was awake, and sometimes even stay with her while she napped so Marion could go for a quick walk.

I proceed past more houses, some familiar and some not. Many are new, replacing old ones or built where none stood before. Now and then a memory-laden one pops up. I pass the home of Ann Gill, who taught us swimming lessons. My dad was an excellent swimmer, as he had been a lifeguard in the past, but his summer work hours were long and his patience was often short, so Ann was hired. I can see her in the water at Homestead, trying to coax me to jump off the dock and into her waiting arms. I wanted her to assure me that not only would she catch me, but that my head would not go under the water. I don't think that ever worked out the way I wished.

On down the road, past the Homestead dock, I see where the Palmers' store once stood. It had a big hall, and I think there might have been dances there at one time. We went there in the winter to get our mail, as the ferry came only that far—and on Tuesdays and Thursdays, there were no ferries at all. This store was also washed away in the '54 hurricane. Marcy Dunbar owns the little store that stands there now. I remember her from my childhood days. When the rest of us were dressed in winter clothing, she would be in shorts, rolling fifty-gallon oil and gasoline drums up the dock all by herself, braids flying in the wind. The parking lot is much bigger now, and the cars, though dusty, all seem to be in relatively good condition, unlike the cars of my memory, which were dilapidated but never left the island for repairs.

My attention turns to the Union Church on the hill above, which was our Protestant summer church. The hill is not as steep nor is the church as large as I remember, but I distinctly recall one Sunday when our usual summer minister Reverend Bob Little was preaching. I had received a Mickey Mouse watch for my sixth birthday in April that year. I was intrigued by my new ability to always know the time. I wore the watch to church and studied it throughout the service, ultimately deciding that Reverend Little had passed the acceptable sermon time limit. As the service wore on, I grew impatient to be outside and swimming on that warm summer day. At the close of the service, he stood at the door greeting everyone and shaking hands as they left. My mother stood right behind me when it was my turn. I looked up at him, tapped the face of my watch, and said, "Your sermon ran a little long today." I'm sure my mother was mortified and would have wished herself into the floorboards if she could. He just smiled, nodded his head, and said, "Thank you for pointing that out. I'll keep it in mind for next week," and on we went.

I ride past what is now the library but was once the Community House, the site of summer ham and bean suppers. Tables lined the front lawn, covered with white paper, and wooden folding chairs were tucked underneath. There were roasting pans filled with home-made baked beans, platters of sliced ham, bowls of tangy potato salad, and whole watermelons, chilling in tubs of ice water, waiting to be cut into juicy, sweet slices for dessert. There were several tables reserved for the penny social, where you could deposit tickets in the cup nearest the items your heart desired and hope your number would be called so you could claim your prize. On the edge of the lawn behind a rope enclosure stood several big metal washtubs filled with water and a plate or two, floating on top. I pitched pennies from outside the rope, hoping to land one or more on the moving plates. If I were successful, I would win a prize. One year, I think I won a tiny teddy bear, and the penny social yielded a new little pink seersucker nightgown for my doll, Rosebud. I was thrilled! But even when I didn't win a prize, it was a festive summer event.

I press on beyond the community called Homestead toward the north end, passing Harriet Cram's house high on the hill, beyond my sight. Her front yard was always a riot of color from her over-flowing summer gardens, and I loved their brilliance. Perhaps that garden and my grandmother's tangled one are the reasons I now love the colorful chaos of my own cottage garden.

Next to appear on the left is the house that once belonged to Dr. Ross, our summer doctor. Island living was sometimes a challenge, especially if medical treatment was needed when the doctor was on the mainland—or if a true emergency arose. Because he was trained in first aid, my dad was often called for minor incidents, especially in the winter. I remember the year that doctors came from the main-land to inoculate all the children for whooping cough—perhaps there had been an outbreak. I also remember the day when I had a painful stomach ache and fever. My dad decided it was quite possibly appendicitis, and he didn't think "wait and see" was a safe option. It was not a day that the ferry ran, so the Coast Guard was summoned. They took my parents and me to Bristol where Dr. Clark saw me immediately. Thankfully it was not appendicitis, but rather it was an infection that responded to an injection of antibiotics or whatever medicine they gave me. When the Coast Guard returned us to the island, I had sufficiently improved to enjoy the adventure.

There are many houses along the way where once there were only fields or woods. It was a part of the island I didn't see very often unless we were going to the Braytons' at the north end. I think the Braytons were the caretakers for the Garland estate, and Ben Brayton was also a fisherman. Their two younger boys, Charlie and Johnny, were in school with my sister and me. The oldest two, Benny and David, were out of school before I began, but Roger was there for one year when I was, when he was in the eighth grade. They also had a little girl, Iris, who was a few years younger than I, and I remember much excitement when she was born into a family of five boys.

I see the road leading to Indian Spring, a fresh water spring where judicious digging sometimes produced Indian arrowheads. One summer day, my mother took us on a walk there. The journey out was fine, but the journey home in the hot sun seemed endless. My mother kept us going by having us sing, "I've ninety-nine miles to go, walk a mile and rest a while, ninety-eight miles to go." I later learned the "Ninety-Nine Bottles of Beer" version, but my mother would never sing something like that, especially not in our presence.

The road I ride now is still dirt, but it seems quite wide, as there is room for two cars to just make it past each other in opposite directions. The road I remember was barely wide enough for one car, and it was really just two tire ruts with grass growing in between and bushes scraping the sides of the car as you drove by. In the spring, it was often impassable because of the deep mud. I reach the short path, now called Chase Way, which leads to Sandy Beach. Today, the brisk, on-shore breeze makes the waves very vocal. There are lines of whitecaps racing along the edge of the shore, each one flowing into the next until they disappear in the shells and sand. Most days when

I come here, it is so quiet, and the clear water of the protected cove is lapping softly along the shore. I think it would be a perfect spot for swimming with little ones, but we never came here. We always went to the Horseshoe—a rough, stony spot where we swam off the rocks. I remember asking my mother as an adult, "Why didn't we ever swim at Sandy Beach?"

"I don't know," she replied after some thought. "The Horseshoe was always our swimming spot. That's just the way it was."

As I leave the path leading to Sandy Beach to complete the last leg of my journey around the island, the bay is hidden once again. I catch a brief glimpse of it and then suddenly it all reappears, an unending ribbon of blue in my vision. I think of those glimmers of water that have appeared and disappeared from my view as I pedaled around the island and decide they are like the people that were part of my life during those early growing up years. Many of the adults were acquaintances, and though always there, they were just a glimmer. Others like Pete and Louise, Millie and Todd, Nana and Grampa Homan, and even Paul and Lois Chapman, the visiting minister and his wife, were as much like extended family as my grandmother was, surrounding me with their nurturing support like the bay surrounds the island. I was raised and loved not only by my parents, but also by the people of this small island community, each one having a part in the person I became.

Island Treasure

The deep blue water is relatively calm this early morning. The tiny waves chatter over an outcropping of rocks off to my right, but in front of me, the waves are barely more than a ripple as they whisper over the larger rocks just below where I sit. I am on the deck of my friend's house, overlooking St. John's Bay. I could easily be on Prudence Island, except for the many lobster traps in front of me and the sound of a lobster boat as it draws closer. It travels down the line, pulling and emptying full traps and then resetting them. This is what lets me know for sure that I am on Pemaquid Point, Maine,

and not Prudence Island, Rhode Island. Yet, the peaceful sounds of the lapping water and the distant gulls carry me back to another summer day I remember on Prudence Island.

— • —

I stepped off the ferry at Homestead expecting to see Judy and Bud Little or Judy alone, waiting to meet me. Instead, it was only Bud, and I wondered where Judy was. We carried my bags to the car, and I sensed an impatience in him. He seemed about to burst, and when he could contain himself no longer, he said excitedly, "I have a surprise for you!" He couldn't wait to show me the surprise, so instead he told me about it. "I cut the path by the ice pond!"

He went on to explain that he first cut the larger brush and then, taking his lawn mower, he worked a little at a time to open the path all the way from the west side by the twin cottages to the driveway leading to my old house. It went past the ice pond where my grandfather used to cut ice in the winter. As we walked down the newly opened path together, our feet released the pungent aroma of dried pine needles warmed by the sun.

I saw the images of two little girls running toward me from the shadows. They were both wearing bathing suits with towels draped on their shoulders; one had dark hair, and the other, blonde curls. There was a youthful joy in their step and excitement in their voices. This was the shortcut my sister Patsy and I took to go to the west side to swim with Judy and other summer friends. The little girls ran through my mind and released a cascade of long-forgotten memories.

Ten years ago, I never thought of writing a book, but then there was a dramatic change in my life. My mother, Evelyn Kaiman, died on November 28, 2005. The following summer, my sister Pat and I wanted to return to Prudence in her memory. After searching for rentals, we finally settled in for a week at Judy and Bud Little's. Although I had not seen Judy for almost sixty years, I felt like we had seen each other yesterday. We resumed our friendship easily, just a slightly older version. I also knew Bud as a child, and I found again a friend in him as well. I returned to the island several times that summer, and many more times in the succeeding years.

When I first returned to Prudence, I felt sad—not only from the pain of my mother's death, but because I felt, once again, like there was nothing here that was mine ... no house, no store, no cottage or place to belong. I had been feeling for years that there was something missing, but I didn't know what. Was it part of me? Or something I was supposed to do? I found that the more I visited Prudence, the more memories I discovered. It was like a treasure box that was locked and placed on a shelf sixty years ago. There it sat, unopened, untouched and gathering dust, buried under piles of stuff. Judy's and Bud's friendship and care revealed the misplaced key to the treasure box. When I opened it, I found the pieces of a jigsaw puzzle that was me. I took the pieces out and began to examine them, one by one. I found some that were missing for so long, just as they were, unharmed by so many years in hiding. There were happy memories filled with light and sunshine that I wanted to hold close. There were also brittle, more-painful ones that I would sooner have left in the box, but I needed them all to finally make the puzzle complete. As the memories emerged, they demanded to be acknowledged, like impatient children wanting their turn on the swing. So many memories released by a walk down a forgotten path. Bud wasn't a man given to emotional demonstrations, but the clearing of that path as a surprise for me was a wordless gift that spoke of his friendship and care. I treasure it still, and am touched every time I think of it, especially since that summer was the last he spent on Prudence Island.

— • —

I am not a historian, and this is not a history book. It is a love story, an answer to the siren's call, a whisper of long-ago unacknowledged loss, pain, and grief, and ultimately, the healing realization that some things in life endure forever. Memories of love and friendships made through the years are mine. They were not washed away with a hurricane or sold with a house. They don't require ownership of land or a street address; they only need room in my heart and my mind to be with me wherever I go. I am drawn to the sea and the salt air and the memories they evoke—from Pemaquid, Maine, to Pensacola, Florida—but no place imparts a healing balm of peace and fulfillment to me like Prudence Island. This story is the gift I was given as I traveled this journey home.

Made in the USA
Middletown, DE
27 June 2021

42963768R00091